There's a Rainbow in Every Snowflake

A Memoir of a Mom's Journey with God

Amy E. Osgood

Copyright

Copyright © 2020 Amy Osgood

All rights reserved. This book or any portion thereof may not be reproduced or used in any manner without the expressed written permission of the publisher.

Some names and identifying details have been changed to protect the privacy of individuals.

Unless otherwise indicated, all scripture quoted from The New Living Translation (NLT) Holy Bible

Editing by Annie Hilbert and Aaron Osgood

Cover Design by Jon Hogge. Rainbows contributed by Rebecca Osgood (First Grade Artwork)

Printed in the United States of America

First Printing 2020

ISB number 978-0-578-63383-1

Dedication

To God, the true Author of my story. And to Rebecca and Jonathon, I am blessed to be called your mom.

Acknowledgements

It takes a village, or in my case, a massive army. Thank you to…

Rebecca and Jonathon, who bravely allowed me to share their stories. Rebecca, this book would have no meaning if you had not called me out on the missing pieces. You will always be one of my best sounding boards. Jonathon, your first reaction to the book idea was foundational for me. Many times over, your faith in me was more than I deserved.

Aaron, my faithful husband. You picked up slack when I was overwhelmed with this project. Thank you for giving me the space to do this, on my terms, staying silent when I didn't need opinions, and bringing the red-editing pen when I did need opinions. Aside from God, your voice will always speak the loudest to me.

Annie Hilbert, my dear friend. How could I have ever done this without you? You were the only one who could say the hard things to me that were total truth and freedom. Thank you for making me not apologize for who I am or for the life I've lived. That conversation didn't just change the book; it changed me.

Jon Hogge, whose perfect blend of let's see what God does and let's get things done, made the book cover happen. Graphic arts and creativity will never be in my wheelhouse; I need you. Thank you! Do you like how I used a semicolon in your section?

Linda, whose face sat across from me over a cup of coffee or a plate of sushi time and again. I would not be the mom I am if you had not been in my life. Your encouragement, friendship, and constant reminder of who I am in Christ has meant everything. The world thanks you, for without you I'd be a mess.

Karrie, my dear friend and neighbor. Before I ever told a soul about this book idea, I found myself telling you about it on a neighbor's deck. Your open mind and great questions prodded me. I still have the tree you drew me that night. I am more than I can see. You told me that.

Grace, the miles we've walked together as moms! I thank you for your simple suggestion to voice record. Apparently, I can't type and cry very well. All of chapter nine was done because of your creative idea. It set me free. And your face when I shared what I thought the title should be brought me confirmation. The Holy Spirit uses you over and over in my life for conviction and confirmation.

Joni, for your hospitality. It was at your cabin that I decided it was worth doing the hard work to make this book right, to finish it, and to tell my story.

Table of Contents

Welcome	I
Chapter 1 – What's My Title?	1
Chapter 2 – Follow Me	23
Chapter 3 – Mysterious Artist	37
Chapter 4 – Self, Less	49
Chapter 5 – Freedom	71
Chapter 6 – Leaning In	91
Chapter 7 – Into the Darkness	119
Chapter 8 – Letting Go	149
Chapter 9 – Redemption	165
Chapter 10 – Mama Osgood	195
Epilogue	211
Notes	212

Welcome

Why would a mom, who has no desire to be a writer, want to put the time, tears, and energy into writing a book? The answer lies within in a story. In late May of 2018, my younger child was just weeks away from graduating high school. The words "empty nesting" swirled around us wherever we went. One particular day that May I was walking along my favorite paved trail in town. As spring trees bloomed all around me and the White River traveled with me on my right, I hiked in silence, but deep in thought. Memories of my children were bouncing all over my mind. A memory would return and I would giggle out loud. Other memories would return to me that made me cringe and my throat tighten with emotion.

Then, out of nowhere, the thought rang perfectly clear in my head: "Put it in a book." It was as though this sentence completely bypassed the logic center of my brain and went straight to my heart. Without thought or acknowledgment, I found myself crying. By this point in my journey with God, I had learned that when something bypasses all reason but draws out a visceral reaction, it is important to pay attention. After that, the memories faded and I spent the rest of the walk telling God that I really didn't want to write a book. I stated my case with clear evidence to Him, why this was a bad idea. But in God's perfect way, He reminded me on that walk along the river that I had spent most of my motherhood wondering if I mattered. I wondered if He or if anyone was paying attention to me. I had feared that motherhood, and the sacrifices that go with it, wouldn't be worth it. I guess, you will have to read the book to decide if I discovered if God was paying attention, if I have value, or if it was worth it. Maybe you have had similar questions? Maybe we have something in common?

Fast forward a few months. Writing was frustrating, which meant it was time to pray more and write less. It was an unseasonably cold November morning. I witnessed "diamond dust" formed by freezing moisture in the air on this cloudless, cold day. As I sat there, contemplating this, a snowflake floated up against my home office window. In a fraction of a moment, the sunlight hit it just right. There it was: a rainbow—tiny—but vividly captured. For reasons unknown to me, tears immediately stung my eyes. I marveled at the truth but also the paradox. *Of course, a rainbow can be inside a snowflake,* I mused to myself. Snowflakes are made of water and when mists of water connect with the sun, a rainbow is created. However, snowflakes come in cold, unfruitful, dead seasons. Not much grows in the snow. Snowflakes are often associated with stillness and inactivity. Snowflakes are small, and, though unique, they easily blend in with the others around them. We know they are temporary and fragile; they melt immediately on our skin. They are gone as quickly as they appear.

Rainbows, on the other hand, are mostly seen in the warm, growing times of the year. Unlike snowflakes, rainbows are huge, spanning the entire sky. Rainbows are unexpected and untouchable. Rainbows offer us hope. A hope of something beautiful yet to come. A hope that something new is on the way. That mid-November, there it was, just outside my window: a snowflake and a rainbow perfectly coexisting.

That beautiful paradox is my life. I am that small, fragile snowflake. God has been full of promise and growth, even when I've felt like nothing was there. When His Son hit my life, a promise of hope grew inside. HE has surprised me with a life of truth, discovery, and unlikely parallels. It's a simple life, but it's a life made remarkable by Jesus. Welcome to the story of my motherhood and my God.

When I first began writing, a thought plagued me, *There are very few people who choose this life of a stay-at-home parent. How will people be able to relate to my story?* Then our entire world was turned upside down by COVID-19. The isolation and uncertainty, financial fears, and questions about how important our work is to us became a global condition. We have all had the order to "stay-at-home," and it has left many asking the questions I wrestled with throughout my entire motherhood. Maybe we aren't as different as I once believed.

We may vary in opinions, in beliefs, and in circumstances, but we have this in common: we have an innate need to know who we are and to know the God who created us. I hope you find yourself relating in the pages ahead. Life really is just a journey to discover God, and by discovering God, we find ourselves.

I invite you to walk around in my shoes for a bit. A little explanation and introduction can go a long way in understanding one another. My world has been small. I grew up in the rural Midwest, and small-town America was all I knew. After graduating college and getting married, I ended up a suburbanite. How's that for basic demographics?

With some convincing, my husband and I mutually decided early in our marriage that, when the time came for children, I would be a homemaker. I had no idea what this one decision would do to my self-worth and my identity. I spent 20 years at home raising our two children, Rebecca and Jonathon. To clarify, I did have a brief season of direct sales (home parties), and for the last several years I have worked for my husband's small business, but I never brought money into our home. I never had a career or an income post children. Even though I have done my fair share of "work," I have not contributed to our family financially. This is the lens God used to help me discover myself and to discover Him.

What else do you need to know? I am a Christian, but let's use the phrase, "I follow Jesus." It is true that once I was lost, but now I am found; however, growing in a relationship with Jesus has been a sloppy journey, not a hymn for me. I'm a hot mess, and God and I both know it. His delight in me and His love for me are greater than my mistakes. I am the one who forgets that, not Him.

Something else we need to discuss, just so we understand one another, is the word sin. This ugly word will be tossed around in the pages ahead. It will prove helpful to clarify what I mean when I bring up sin. Richard Rohr, a Franciscan friar from Albuquerque, New Mexico, defines sin as "fixations that prevent the energy of life, God's love, from flowing freely. Sin is *self-erected blockades* that *cut us off from God* and hence from our own authentic potential." [Emphasis mine] This definition goes far beyond God's do's and don'ts. Please, keep that in mind as you read.

Both my family of origin—and the family I married into—have had their share of divorce, abuse, addiction, trauma, and estranged relationships. It is not a perfect life that afforded me a relationship with Jesus. It is the imperfect nature of my life that led me to Jesus. My daily challenge is to live out of His example: His love, His mercy, His grace, His forgiveness. Success varies from day to day. Without fail, God continues to teach me to look at myself and embrace that I am His beautiful mess.

How are you doing? Have I fallen into any stereotypes yet? In case I have, so we understand one another, let me make a couple clarifications about marriage and work:

- Marriage - Far from perfect. While I am married to an amazing man who is sacrificial, who is a very intentional husband, and who is a highly involved father, he and I are both very broken people who have taken that brokenness out on each other. We brought pain, mistakes, and fear from our individual lives (see above family histories), and we put them together in marriage. What else would you expect? We fight like all the rest of you about money, sex, and how to raise our children. Only those very close to us know where we have struggled in marriage. In an effort to honor each other, we have kept our fights and disagreements relatively private. The absence of those arguments in this book does not mean they didn't happen. That's just not the story I'm going to tell in these pages. But, if you're curious, we've been married for 26 years and we have a lifetime to go.
- Work - In the beginning, our decision for me to be a stay-at-home mom was accepted and

even encouraged. As the kids got older and entered elementary school, middle school, and then high school, I heard opposition both directly stated and implied: "Why doesn't Amy get off her butt and help out?" and "Those kids don't need a parent at home anymore." Some people were concerned that I may not have any skills or experience to offer an employer after giving up two decades to be at home. Judgments are easy to make from a distance. No one knows our whole story. This might not sound like a big deal, but it has been a thorn in my side. Who am I if I don't have a job?

Do I matter? Is anyone paying attention to me? Is it worth it? Allow me to open the door. I invite you to step into my world.

Chapter 1
What's My Title?

You saw me before I was born. Every day of my life was recorded in your book. Every moment was laid out before a single day had passed.

Psalm 139:16

The most significant woman in my world was my mom. My childhood included two working parents—dad was an agricultural businessman who sold seed to farmers and my mom was a nurse. Although dad worked from home, he traveled daily to farmers in his region and held district sales meetings that required late hours. When he wasn't traveling, he was on the phone. Dad provided well for our family, but it demanded a lot of him. My mom had a long season of being a school nurse when my older brother and sister were in middle school. Mom also worked in hospitals, in doctor's offices, and in people's homes as a visiting nurse. When I was 15, she returned to college to get her Master's Degree in Counseling. My mom was a strong, smart woman who worked hard for what she wanted, and she provided excellent healthcare to those entrusted to her.

I went off to college with the plan to eventually work with children and families with the same drive, integrity, and know-how my mom exemplified. But just a few months before I left home, my older sister had her first child—my first niece. Maybe it was my sister's example or my age when a baby entered our family, but maternal instincts were taking deep root in me, even then. Part of me wanted a baby, eventually, but I told myself I had things to do and lives to change first.

My internal conflict probably began in the college classroom. As an Individual and Family Development major, I learned a lot about child development, family dynamics, social science, and psychology. Back then, in the late 80's and early 90's, women's careers were on the rise, driving the need for quality child care options. For four years I wrestled academically with family structure, demographics, and child mental, physical, and emotional health. I wanted a career. I wanted to make a difference and support families. But, what did that mean for me? What would be best for *my* children? I considered these things well before a husband and kids were in the picture.

At the end of my sophomore year of college, I met my future husband, Aaron, and everything was shaping up for this significant, comfortable life I had planned in my head. Before I even held my diploma in my hand, I had secured a job as a Program Director for the YMCA. Amy's must-do list: get a Bachelor's of Science degree from a Big Ten university. Check. Start a career working with children and families. Check. Get married. Check. Everything was going according to plan.

As a Program Director for the YMCA, approximately 25 part-time employees ultimately reported to me. That meant I interviewed people frequently, since part-time childcare had high turnover in this job. I learned at the YMCA that I really liked interviewing people, finding out what they wanted, and hopefully making a match.

The nonprofit world was losing its luster, and I longed for a more corporate job. Eventually, I ended up working in Human Resources for Charles Schwab, a large investment company. While I worked at Schwab, the desire for children grew from a flicker into a red-hot flame. I loved my job. I loved interviewing and hiring people. I loved getting them acclimated to our work culture, but my longing to be a mom was overpowering. Furthermore, I really wanted to stay at home and just be mom.

Conversations with Aaron weren't always easy during this season. We both had a lot of concerns about finances. He worked in the nonprofit and not-for-profit world. We weren't exactly rolling in cash. This was in the 90's. Technology was in most homes, but options for working from home were in very short supply. Crisis point: I wanted desperately to be a stay-at-home mom, and I also wanted to feel important and purposeful. Dreams came true and expectations were shattered all at the same time.

Once Aaron got on board with becoming a father and with me staying at home, we discovered that getting pregnant isn't necessarily easy. Our OB/GYN told us one of the problems was stress. My workload was demanding, especially during massive hiring seasons. Among the HR staff, we referred to these seasons as "cattle calls" because we would hire so many employees at once for the call center. Knowing I would eventually quit this job to stay at home with the baby—whenever it came along—I went to my boss to tell her that I needed to drop to 30 hours a week. I was an energetic, industrious 26-year-old about to tell my supervisor that I wanted to be a mommy. She however, was a corporate, business-minded woman in her mid-40's, married, and without children. I believe her name was Kay. I walked into her office, my heart pounding, throat tight, and afraid of what she'd think of me. Kay sat with her body turned to the side as she worked on her computer. When I asked if she had a minute, she turned, body straight at her desk, folded her arms, and looked directly up at me. I didn't sit down. I remained standing to cover up feeling so small. I don't know Kay's story or why she did not have children, but I feared her judgment of my desire to have a family. I took a deep breath and choked out, "Kay, I need to decrease my hours to 30 a week. My husband and I are trying to get pregnant, and it seems that too much stress is a part of the problem."

I worked on contract with Schwab, so I didn't need her permission. However, I wanted to have integrity, and I did care about the work I was doing. Kay took the information, and we figured out what hours and days of the week would work for both of us. It was professional and very business focused. All my emotional, inner yearnings sat outside the room like a package sits on the doorstep. When I left her office, she spoke this prophetic statement: "Amy, the only important words on your tombstone will say 'wife and mother.' It won't list your job on it." I closed her office door, picked up my invisible box of emotions and desires, and pressed on.

Now may the God of peace make you holy in every way, and may your whole spirit and soul and body be kept blameless until our Lord Jesus Christ comes again. God will make this happen, for he who calls you is faithful.

1 Thessalonians 5:23-25

Within about six months of that conversation with Kay, we got pregnant. Our first baby's arrival into this world approached; I was excited and had all sorts of expectations. I would quit work. The house would get vacuumed every other day. We would go for walks. Surely, I would have to find things to do because babies sleep all the time. Aaron and I would probably need to find a church and actually start attending. That's what is expected, right? We clean up the kids and present a happy little family!? Yes, this is what my life would be like. Tidy. Easy.

Where was I with God at this point in my life? I had been praying and asking for a baby, but that was about it. I believed in Jesus and said I was a Christian. But I didn't regularly attend church, read the Bible or even consider God. Most of the time I decided what I wanted and only checked in with Him whenever my expectations weren't being met.

Because I wanted to be the best stay-at-home mom I could be, I read *What to Expect When You're Expecting*, dog-earring page after page. Breastfeeding was supposed to be best for the baby, so that's what I'd do. I took very good care of myself during the pregnancy with the exception of a few too many chocolate milkshakes. I told myself the baby craved it. Besides, it made me feel better because she would kick incessantly once that thick chocolaty joy passed through the umbilical cord. It was a win-win! Between the planning and the milkshakes, I really did enjoy my first pregnancy.

One night in May of 1998, Rebecca entered the narrative of our life. It was a long labor but no major complications. All the healthy habits I exercised while I was pregnant, I continued as I breastfed. Technically, whatever I ate, she ate, so I was mindful of what I was ingesting. But even the best decisions and plans can backfire.

On the very first day home from the hospital, all the pre-baby daydreams about staying at home exploded. A few hours into the evening, baby Rebecca was screaming, and wailing, and simply DID NOT STOP. I assumed she must be hungry, but I could not get her latch on. All she would do was scream and fight at my breast. For hours and hours, she wailed right through every feeding and every nap. Newborns eat and sleep—that's all, right? The first night at home, Rebecca was up for 13 hours straight! I was pretty sure I had managed to break my baby within hours of being sent home. I called the nursery at the hospital because it was the middle of the night, and we were a wreck. They said, "Oh, she just probably has a little gas." *A little gas? Are you kidding? No, I'm pretty sure my baby knows that I have no idea as to what I'm doing,* rumbled the thoughts in my head.

What's My Title?

Rebecca had cried nonstop all night. I was exhausted, desperate, and so sad that I couldn't help her. I paced the floor carrying my weeping child. We tried the rocking chair, the recliner, her crib. We went back and forth, trying to feed her and trying to soothe her. Clearly, I was clueless, so we decided to follow the instruction from the nurses at the hospital. If it is gas, it's gotta get out! You can't force a baby to burp, so Aaron went hunting in the midnight hours for a 24-hour drug store to buy Mylicon drops. The drops are supposed to break down the gas in babies' tummies. Aaron returned with the treasure in his hand. Just before dawn, we finally had a successful feeding. I buttoned her up in my pajama shirt and lay with her on my chest in our recliner. I was afraid of sleeping with an infant due to my research, but the hospital said it was safe in our situation. Fulfilling all the instructions from the night nurse, we both fell asleep.

The lactation consultant called us later the next day when she heard from the other hospital staff about our midnight call. She asked me what I ate the day before. I was overly defensive as I told her what I ate, assuring her it was completely healthy!! With a matter-of-fact tone in her voice she said, "Oh, you ate a banana." A banana? Seriously? A harmless piece of fruit made her wail all night long? Apparently, bananas have high gas-producing qualities, and babies can't always break it down. I wish *that* was in the book! I ate healthy and *still* got it wrong! Little did I know this was just the beginning…

It turned out that Rebecca was a baby with colic. The days were filled with intense, all-day crying; evenings and nights were no better. Even now, I still grieve her first few months of life. She was so miserable, no matter what I did, and I couldn't fix it for her. That is just the way our story unfolded. After taking a week off when Rebecca was born, my husband returned to work, and I was left alone in my new job as stay-at-home mom. A couple weeks into our "new normal" Aaron entered through the back door after work. The house was quiet which was a rarity. I'm sure he thought he was walking into the wrong house. All he could see was the back of my head over the top of my grandmother's old rocking chair. Wisely, he walked in quietly, assuming Rebecca was nursing or napping. I'm pretty sure he was hoping for a scene of his beautiful wife, peacefully feeding his baby girl. Instead, there I was in stained pajamas, and my hair was still in the half-undone ponytail from the night before. Mind you, it was about 6 o'clock in the evening. He silently walked around to stand in front of me. There, he found my face streaked with tears and sweat. The smell of dried breastmilk hung in the air. He looked down at Rebecca in my arms who was not nursing. Instead, she finally fell asleep after finding her own toe to suck on. Aaron, of course, thought this was the cutest thing ever. I could see a sentimental expression growing on his face. My face? Well, blades of fire were shooting from my eyes as I mouthed, "Do not get cheesy right now. If you're smart, you'll just turn and walk away." I just sat there in my failure to comfort my child. This is exactly where I started from. Clueless. Broken. Every hopeful expectation shattered. Failing at my new job. If I had been worthy of a business card, it would have looked something like this:

After trying for years to get pregnant with Rebecca, our son, Jonathon came as a big surprise. Although a second child was always the plan, my plan included putting another year between the children. I was just getting the hang of having a little one around. Rebecca's colic was under control, and she was full of life and fun. My pregnancy with Jonathon was not as easy as Rebecca's. I had morning sickness for the first six months, one good month, and then with eight weeks left of pregnancy, I went into preterm labor. After a couple days in the hospital, I was forced to go on bedrest, with a 22-month old at home. My mom worked. My sister lived an hour and a half away. I had no help, and I couldn't take care of both Rebecca and in-utero Jonathon. Fortunately, my best friend from college got Rebecca a temporary spot at her child's daycare. I would lie on the couch feeling like I failed because Rebecca wasn't at home with me, and my body was trying to kick Jonathon out too soon.

Knowing my situation, my OB/GYN scheduled to induce labor one week before the due date. The baby was healthy and ripe, and I had a family to take care of. I labored for hours with Rebecca, but Jonathon burst onto the scene of our family in June of 2000. He, too, was an uncomplicated delivery. However, within hours of his birth, just as I dozed off, he made a horrific sound from his bedside hospital crib. I shot up from sleep. *Ouch! Don't move so fast Amy.* I hit the call button for a nurse.

There was a brief moment in the delivery room when the doctor told me not to push. I didn't have an epidural and my body said "push." I tried to back-peddle in the stirrups but couldn't help it and pushed anyway.

Jonathon came out quickly, before the doctor could aspirate his mouth. He ended up with fluid in his lungs. There in his bedside crib, infant Jonathon hacked out the fluid from his lungs. It was not a sound we expected to hear. Within hours of entering our world, Jonathon was diagnosed with acid reflux. We were told he should grow out of it during his first year of life. He may have not cried and wailed like Rebecca did, but as an infant he would projectile vomit, sometimes after feedings and sometimes for no apparent reason. Baby Jonathon was smiles and contentment…and a lot vomit.

When Jonathon was just two months old, we took the kids to the Indiana State Fair in August. We had been at the fair for about 20 minutes, when we stopped to watch the cloggers dance. Without warning Jonathon hurled all over my shoulder, dousing my hair. My shirt was soaked, and my hair was drenched in regurgitated baby formula. Yes, I continued to walk the fairgrounds that day with dried baby vomit brewing in the Indiana heat and humidity. That day taught me to pack his diaper bag with two or three extra outfits for him and a fresh shirt and hair tie for me.

When Rebecca was born, Aaron took a week off. When Jonathon was born, he only took a couple days off. Here's how that conversation went. We were eating dinner; Rebecca was perched in her highchair and Jonathon was napping in a bouncy seat. As a forkful of food was on its way to my mouth, (no, it was not a banana) Aaron said, "I think I'll go back to work tomorrow." I didn't even look at him. I put the fork down, scooted the chair away from the table, walked upstairs, and began to sob. After securing the kids, Aaron followed me and asked, "What's the matter?" No kidding, this is what I said to him, "What am I supposed to do with two of them—all day—by myself?" I was scared to death of handling a two-year-old and a five-day-old. Surely, I would be found out yet again: I had no idea what I was doing. And this was supposed to be my job!

I thought being a stay-at-home mom would be important. I thought it would be rewarding. I definitely thought I'd be better at it than I was. Staying at home with two little ones revealed that I was clueless, broken and needed God more than ever. I was grumpy, lonely, selfish, and losing my sense of purpose.

Thankfully, when Rebecca was an infant, God had already planted a seed of a thought in my head. My sister told me about the *Left Behind*[1] book series, a best-selling Christian fictional novel series with an interpretation of the Biblical apocalypse. One of the main characters, Buck Williams, was attempting to contact co-workers after worldwide mass disappearances. He came across the son of a co-worker who told Buck with confidence where his mom was. Her love of Jesus was evident: he knew that she was in heaven. This idea of knowing Jesus with such confidence held itself over me like a speech bubble. Baby Rebecca lay in my arms as I read. I looked down at her sweet little face. *What will she say about me when we're older? Will there be a story of God in my life?* Little did I know, Jesus would hide that seedling in the dark soil of my soul until it was time to start growing.

Aaron and I eventually found our church home, Grace Church, when Rebecca was three and Jonathon was one. This was a game changer for me. Grace gave me solid biblical teaching, a place to serve, community, and a way to discover my own relationship with Jesus. But at home, I struggled with feeling insignificant, and I made a lot of mistakes. So, from time to time, I looked for work.

I wanted a job to escape my own parenting troubles, and I was beginning to believe that childcare workers could raise my kids better than I could. I also wanted a job because I wanted to know that I was important and that I mattered. Once, I applied to work at our church in the ministry in which I regularly volunteered. I made it through the screening process, but before the interview, I had a pivotal conversation with a friend. She knew my struggles as I wore the title of stay-at-home mom, so she poked at me to uncover my motives.

At the heart of it, I was tired of not having an answer for "What do you do?" I wanted to let other people know I had value, skills, and a proper title. My friend never told me what to do, but her words still ring in my ears: "Just because you *can* do the job, doesn't mean that you *should* do the job." It was enough for me to pause, circle back around to God, and ask HIM. *God, is this what You want me to do?* To no surprise, I withdrew my name, and continued the silent, hidden work in our home. The stay-at-home journey was God's way of inviting me into a world where I would have to learn that my meaning would not be found in income, prestige, or title. Hidden inside the walls of my home, that's where my meaning and purpose would grow and be discovered.

Despite all my many shortcomings, I did have a very strong maternal instinct. The mommy gene was in full force by the time Jonathon was fifteen months old. The doctors were concerned that he hadn't out-grown his acid reflux yet. They wanted to take a deeper look to see if anything else was going on in his tummy. We brought him to a pediatric gastroenterologist, and she scheduled him for an endoscopy. The doctor allowed us to be in the room when they put him under anesthesia. I smiled and stayed strong until his little eyes were closed. Then I walked outside the door, leaned hard against the wall, and started to weep. The doctor came out and said, "Good job, Mom! I passed out when I saw my kid go under—and I'm a doctor." We were told it wouldn't be long but to grab a bite to eat, and they'd come get us.

Aaron and I walked in silence to the cafeteria and got lunch. As we walked back to the waiting room, I heard it. A child's cry. Not just any child. MY CHILD! I could hear Jonathon screaming, but I couldn't get to him. I picked up the pace, blankly repeating to Aaron, "That's Jonathon. That's Jonathon."

We ran to the nurse's station and said, "That's my child! He's awake. We're supposed to be there."

She calmly replied, "Did they call your name?"

"No, but *he's* calling my name. I'm MOMMY!!"

Finally, we ran into his recovery area. Jonathon was groggy from the anesthesia and was as mad as a hornet. He had partially yanked out the IV in his arm and blood was everywhere. His arm, his pale-yellow surgery gown, and his sheets all painted with blood. By the time we reached the recovery room, I was pretty bossy, and I couldn't have cared less about protocol. I grabbed him from the bed and sat down, so he could be close to my heart and rest his head in the familiar safety of my neck. The nurse told me to put him down so she could get the IV out.

"Uh, NO! You can get it from here."

I may have made a lot of mistakes, but I had old-cow-syndrome. This is how my farming family referred to the over-protectiveness and complete disorientation the mother experiences when she's separated from her child. It is something that heifers do when they can't find their calf. They bawl, kick, and throw a fit, disrupting the entire herd until mama has her calf safely by her side. I may not have had maternal instincts to get the everyday decisions right, but, yes, I was an old cow.

And I am convinced that nothing can ever separate us from God's love. Neither death nor life, neither angels nor demons, neither our fears for today nor our worries about tomorrow – not even the powers of hell can separate us from God's love. No power in the sky above or in the earth below – indeed, nothing in all creation will ever be able to separate us from the love of God that is revealed in Christ Jesus our Lord.

Romans 8:38-39

Could God be an old cow, too, not wanting us to be separated from His love?

Chapter 2
Follow Me

Christ is also the head of the church, which is his body. He is the beginning, supreme over all who rise from the dead. So he is first in everything.

Colossians 1:18

In the early years of motherhood, most of my learning about God was thanks to the *VeggieTales* DVD series. Those computer-animated stories hosted by Bob the Tomato and Larry the Cucumber allowed my then nearly thirty-year-old self to understand the different events of the Bible. It was important to me that my kids learn the stories, but watching *VeggieTales* revealed to me how little I knew. I was learning right alongside my children.

There was no shame as I grew in my knowledge of God. Aaron and I started connecting at church. God brought people into my life who walked with me at a pace I could keep. Jesus ascended up my priority list. Still, the question that the *Left Behind* book raised, *What am I all about?*, would return to me every few years.

My son was a perfect analogy, and it got my attention. When Jonathon was three years old, he was all about trains. Everywhere he went, he had a train car in his hand. It was likely that he had trains on his underwear, too. If you were to pass him in the store or to see him at preschool, he would tell you all about what the train cars were hauling and how they fit together. Jonathon was all about trains; you couldn't miss that about him. I had been learning Bible stories, and I was volunteering at church, but that wasn't enough. Was I "all-in" for Jesus the way Jonathon was "all-in" with his trains? I felt Jesus' nudge on my shoulder: *I can see, Child, that you now understand to follow Me, but look behind you. Your children are following you. What do you have to offer them?*

Rebecca had always been a fearful child and was quite timid in unfamiliar circumstances. Because of this, she was my shadow—wherever I was, she was. I never left her sight. To an emotionally healthy, patient mom, this could be a bit frustrating, but to someone like me who wanted to be "in control of everything" and "independent," this was maddening! I loved her to the ends of the earth, but I could not handle being with her all the time, not because of who *she* was, but because of who *I* was. I thought that if she were different, or if I could change her, then I'd be OK. I'm pretty confident God laughed aloud when He saw me living out that lie. Changing *other people* never makes *me* better! If God rolls His eyes, He was rolling His eyes at my mixed-up intentions. He was about to set me straight.

One day, I made young Rebecca stay in her bedroom alone to play. She was not being punished; I was just looking for a little personal space. After only a few moments, I neared her door and I stood in the hallway; all I could hear was her was talking to herself. Rebecca was chattering on about where people were in the house and that she was alone in her room, in a hurried, edgy tone. She wasn't playing make-believe—she was fretting in her isolation. In that moment of profound revelation, God allowed me to realize that Rebecca was

EXACTLY like me. I, too, never left my mom's side, and I was out of sorts when separated from her. Separation anxiety had dominated my childhood, and now I had passed down to my daughter the fear that I had forced deep inside myself and covered it up with controlling self-sufficiency. Not only was I terribly saddened by this revelation, I was also keenly aware that I could not help her. I had never gotten out from under the oppressive fear—I had just buried it. I had nothing to offer, no path to show Rebecca the way out. Bankrupt. I wanted so much better for her.

I know I'm not alone in this discovery that as a mom we inadvertently pass down our bondage to our children. I have had several conversations with other moms. An adult woman who still struggled with seasons of bulimia nervosa said, "I hope my daughter doesn't have the horrible body image I had." Another mom wept over the judgmental nature of her teenager, knowing that two sentences prior, she herself had judged someone too harshly. Until we find health and victory for ourselves, we will never be able to help someone else to health and victory, especially our children.

Long ago the LORD said to Israel: "I have loved you, my people, with an everlasting love. With unfailing love I have drawn you to myself.

Jeremiah 31:3

As someone draws water from a deep well, Jesus drew me to Himself. That changed everything. I had moved from being a "Christian" to being a "Christ follower." That day outside Rebecca's bedroom door, Jesus invited me to look into *my* hidden fears and wounds. Jesus was about to take me by the hand and lead me down the path of healing. I was about to go first for my children.

Do you know that scary feeling, when you know change is going to come and the unknown stands before you?

What was I going to discover? What was I going to have to feel? But there was a gentle, loving-kindness that pulled me toward Jesus, and, I soon learned, this is where I'm safest. The road isn't easy, but it is better.

A.W. Tozer said in his book, *The Pursuit of God*:

> We pursue God because, and only because, He has first put an urge within us that spurs us to the pursuit. "No man can come to me," said our Lord, "except the Father which hath sent me draw him" (John 6:44), and it is by this prevenient drawing that God takes from us every vestige of credit for the act of coming. The impulse to pursue God originates with God, but the outworking of that impulse is our following hard after Him. All the time, we are pursuing Him we are already in His hand: "Thy right hand upholdeth me."[2]

Working through emotional and spiritual healing is like going in for surgery. While there is hope to be well on the other side, it is scary. I wanted to be well but at the same time, I had lived my whole life being sick, stuck in patterns of behavior based on lies, pain, and trauma.

That was familiar. I didn't know what to expect from healing. I believe that, for most people, something different, unknown, or unfamiliar is scary.

I have had a few real surgeries over the course of my life. During the surgical process, I am responsible for following directions and trusting those involved. My surgeon was responsible for cutting, removing, or remodeling, and sewing back together. I had a team of nurses and other staff to encourage, rehabilitate, and teach me a new way move and live. Honestly, healing hurts. Healing takes time, and healing requires a lot of relearning.

I had to dig deep within myself to find the courage to get emotional and spiritual healing. Becoming self-aware is a brutal task. Who wants to look at their own sin? Who wants to acknowledge the hurt and fears of childhood? Who really likes to step into the unknown and unrevealed about what lies in the darkness of their heart, their mind, and their past? I had spent my life up to this point self-protecting and "managing" the issues that held me back. With the revelation that I had nothing to offer my kids, except to establish the same broken patterns in them, I decided it was time for me to get well. They were, and always have been, my biggest motivation. The internal plane of my life was going down, and I needed to put on my own oxygen mask before fumbling to put it on my children. I still feel like this is the bravest thing I have ever done. Back then, I was not in a place where I would do it for myself, but for my children I would. That journey has taken decades.

In *Basic Christianity*[3] John Stott writes:

> In the beginning God. The first four words of the Bible are more than a way of launching the story of creation or introducing the book of Genesis. They supply the key that opens our understanding to the Bible as a whole. They tell us that the religion of the Bible is a religion in which *God takes the initiative*. The point is that we can never take God by surprise. We can never anticipate him. He always makes the first

move. He is always there "in the beginning." Before we existed, God took action. *Before we decided to look for God, God had already been looking for us.* The Bible isn't about people trying to discover God but about God reaching out to find us. [Emphasis mine]

Just like there is no formula for finding God, there is no formula for receiving spiritual and emotional healing. The journey is as individual as the person and as uniquely personal as each individual's relationship to God. But these were the three critical components to my healing:

1. The Word of God—Jesus was the surgeon. He did all the cutting, removing, and remodeling. Through Bible study and memorizing verses of truth about God and His view of me, I learned that Jesus rebuilt a solid foundation for me to stand on.

2. Professional Christian Counseling—My seasons in counseling were like physical therapy after an injury. My counseling included a lot of prayer. A LOT OF

PRAYER! Prayer during my counseling session. Prayer during trigger moments. Prayer all the time. Constant communication between me and The Divine One was critical.

3. Being part of a healthy community—This was my rehab staff. I had a small circle of women who were gentle with my heart, prayed for me and with me, and held me accountable. Let's face it, we all need a tribe! Mine was full of love, acceptance, compassion, and truth.

Although God invited me into this healing process, you may be wondering how HE went first for me. Didn't HE just tell me to pull myself together? No, I told myself that. Here is what I learned from the healing of Christ. For all the times and ways people had let me down, Jesus reminded me that His family didn't believe in Him. His friends betrayed and abandoned Him. For every physical pain that I endured, He had a crown of thorns pounded into His head. He was struck with whips tipped with glass and metal. For all the times and ways that I was humiliated or embarrassed, He hung naked on a cross in full public view. For every lie that I believed, He was tempted by the enemy to believe lies BUT resisted them with the truth. He showed me how. For all the times and ways that I felt unheard or disrespected, He was spit on and mocked. For all the times and ways that I thought God forgot me or didn't care, Jesus cried out in my place, "Why have you forsaken me?" so I would never have to be separated from the Father. Jesus went first. And for every sin, intentional or accidental, that I am guilty of, He said, "No, I will take her punishment." Jesus did the one thing I couldn't do for myself: He reconciled me to God.

He was despised and rejected—a man of sorrows, acquainted with deepest grief. We turned our backs on him and looked the other way. He was despised, and we did not care. Yet it was our weaknesses he carried; it was our sorrows that weighed him down. And we thought his troubles were a punishment from God, a punishment for his own sins! But he was pierced for our rebellion, crushed for our sins. He was beaten so we could be whole. He was whipped so we could be healed. Isaiah 53:3-5

Follow Me

He personally carried our sins in his body on the cross so that we can be dead to sin and live for what is right. By his wounds you are healed.

1 Peter 2:24

It is ONLY because of this miraculous healing that Jesus and I worked on together that years later I finally had something to offer my children. When they were toddlers, I couldn't help them find their way. But now, two decades later, because of Christ, I can. The summer before Jon left for his first year at college and Rebecca returned for her junior year, real issues surfaced for both of them. They had become young adults, and their relationships came with very adult feelings: a heartbreak for one and the discouragement of ongoing waiting for the other. Their feelings were real, raw, and exposed. There was NOTHING I could do for their pain. I couldn't brush over it. A bowl of ice cream wouldn't cheer this sadness and uncertainty away. Together in the kitchen, we sat in the emotional mess. We let the painful feelings do their work.

Finally, because of what God had taught me, I could speak truth into the darkness that they found themselves in: "There are three things going on here, kids. The world is telling you what your life should look like now, but that's not God's voice. The enemy is poking at every insecurity you have, but God is building you up, so that when the right person is in the picture, you will want to work at the hard stuff."

I cannot dream or imagine what their adult lives will look like. I don't know the joys and successes they will have. I don't know the challenges and failures that they will endure. But I do know this: God went first for me, led me, and stayed with me. He will go first for them, lead them, and stay with them.

Chapter 3
The Mysterious Artist

Truly, O God of Israel, our Savior, you work in mysterious ways.

Isaiah 45:15

I'm not very good at arts and crafts (sad for a stay-at-home mom). I enjoy doing them, and I try pretty hard, I'm really just not good at it. My mom, however, has done various types of needlework ever since I can remember. Currently in her early eighties, she is serving her church community by crocheting prayer blankets. Several people from her rural church will gather and pray healing prayers over each of the blankets before they are hand-delivered to those in their community who are sick or recovering from surgeries. For those who aren't familiar with crocheting, Mom will take her needles and yarn, sometimes all the same yarn, sometimes yarn of different colors or textures, and she will make several sections. When a section is done, she sets it aside. Once all the sections are complete, she will place each piece where it should go and crochet them all together to complete the blanket. It seems to me God's plans often unfold in the same fashion.

Oh, how great are God's riches and wisdom and knowledge! How impossible it is for us to understand his decisions and his ways!

Romans 11:33

The mystery of God can be unsettling, to say the least. What section of the blanket is He working on, or how long it will be set aside? Will it really even fit in with the other pieces? I have been in and out of these mysterious seasons over and over. Unfortunately, they don't get any easier. As I write this, I am currently sitting in a time of not understanding God and His ways. Feeling weak and uncertain is my "normal" right now. I believe that God is good, faithful, and is working all things out. This believing (right now) requires intentionally rehearsing God's goodness, faithfulness, and sovereignty. Pain and uncertainty blind me to the truth of Jesus. The mystery of God collides with my faith. He makes Himself known, yet I am unable to fully understand Him.

Faith shows the reality of what we hope for; it is the evidence of things we cannot see.

Hebrews 11:1

Rebecca used to watch a PBS children's show called *Between the Lions*. This show was about a family of lions who lived in and worked in a library. Oh, the wonder of puppetry! One episode features an African folk story about two farmer friends who lived across the road from each other. One day, a trickster wears a hat as he travels south and passes between the farmers. One side of the hat is blue, and the other side of the hat is red. After the trickster passes through, the farmers comment on his beautiful hat. They then begin feuding. The farmer on the east side of the road declares that the hat was blue. The farmer on the west side of the road argues that the hat was red. The farmers quarrel all day long until sunset when the trickster traveled back north and passes between them again, this time in the opposite direction. It is at this moment the farmers realize that neither of them could see the hat in its entirety until the end of the day. This little story opened my eyes to see that I rarely have all of the information. I think I'm right, and the facts that I know are all the facts. That leaves very little room for the God of the universe and what HE sees.

God continued to use this African folktale a few years later. I was at church for a Bible study. Round tables were set up with eight chairs around them. In the center of each table was a single box. I can't remember the purpose of the box or what we studied that day. All that I recall is that as I sat at the table, I wondered if the woman across from me was looking at the same thing on her side of the box. Was it the same color as mine? Did it have a design that mine didn't? Were there words? The box had five visible sides. Where someone sat at the table determined what they saw on the box. Then there was that sixth side that was touching the table that no one could see. Was there something that was still a part of the box but remained hidden? I gained great perspective just by acknowledging there is always more than what I can see right in front of me.

Several more years passed until God brought this back to my mind. I was reading *Draw the Circle* by Mark Batterson. This book encourages the reader to figuratively "draw the circle" around an issue that concerns them and then pray around that issue for 40 days or until they see God move on their behalf. Circling a concern in prayer can be stubbornly, persistently talking to God about the issue. There was an issue I had been talking to God about for many, many years. As I was praying around this issue during the 40 day prayer challenge I realized something. I could sit stubbornly in the middle of the circle, but I could also walk around the issue and see it from many different perspectives. I might think I have all the information perched inside my circle, but am I truly able to see every side of an issue? No. Let's also not forget there are some aspects of an issue that God keeps hidden, just like the box on the tabletop.

Yes, this can be unsettling. Frequently, I want all of the information. I wrongly believe that if I have all the information, I would have control. But God has trained me to take heart, for He knows I can't handle the truth, at least not all at once. Anyone else picturing Jack Nicholson yelling, "You can't handle the truth!" from the movie *A Few Good Men*? Yes, God is showing me how to find joy and excitement in not knowing or understanding why some things happen. He is strengthening my confidence in HIM. If I live like I have all the information, then I feel like I'm responsible for all the possible solutions. I don't know about you, but too often I've been in a situation, and I needed Someone bigger, wiser, and more creative than me, simply because I couldn't see a way out with just my own intellect. It is times like those when the mystery of God is a comfort.

God's mysterious nature emerges by Him withholding information, but He is also mysterious by transforming seemingly mundane events into life markers. It's like watching an artist. To a spectator, the process can look careless and haphazard. The artist takes colors and shapes that don't make sense. They keep working but there seems to be no discernable order to the process.

Watching their artwork come to life can seem random and disconnected. Once the artist determines that the image successfully made it to their canvas in its fullness, then they put down the brush and step back to look at what they created. This is how God works. I only get a glimpse of a smudge of paint here or there. I can't get a sense of the image. Not until HE's done can I look back and see it. What was once mysterious, ends up being a beautiful work of artistry. The seemingly insignificant elements are brought together into a masterpiece.

But Jesus replied, "My Father is always working and so am I."
John 5:17

This next story might not seem to fit; it is not even about my children directly. Without this next tale, this book will not make much sense. A benign comment became a turning point; however, I could not see its significance until years later. Oh, the mystery of God. I had no idea what He would do with this moment.

The Mysterious Artist

It was Rebecca's freshman year of high school, and I was chaperoning her show choir's first competition of the season. What is show choir? Simply put, it is a group combining choral singing and dance choreography. A show choir set is about 20 minutes long, often with Broadway or pop-culture themes, a full band, and multiple costume changes. Show choir is mostly prevalent in the Midwest, although there are pockets in other parts of the country where it is popular. High school music programs host large competitions, often with more than 10 different schools competing, as a fundraiser to support their own music program. A competition day often starts before 5 a.m. with a departure from our local school. We haul all the singers, show choir band students, instruments, costumes, and any set pieces and backdrops. For the size of our program, this requires four school buses and a truck that pulls a trailer full of equipment. The days are long. If one of our choirs advances to the final round, all of our choirs stay. Finals usually end around 11:30 p.m., and then we drive home. It can be a 21-hour ordeal, returning to our local school around 1 or 2 a.m. the next morning.

The high school that hosts the competition often utilizes nearly all areas of their building. The cafeteria has meals and snacks to purchase. The library often hosts a solo vocal competition where students can compete with an individual song. Regular classrooms are transformed into home-rooms for each choir. This is where the students get dressed, put on makeup, and get ready to perform.

I had volunteered as a chaperone when Rebecca was in the middle school show choir, but this particular competition was the first for me at the high school level. I didn't know any of the other choir moms who mostly had upperclassmen students. They knew how to chaperone and what competition days looked like at the high school level. So, I just tried to catch on and let others run the day. Our middle school show choir had been well-organized and successful, but the high school's program director lacked leadership and organizational skills (more to come on that later). The stakes were higher in the high school, but the program itself was a step backwards.

Rebecca's choir met in a classroom which quickly became lined with desks covered in make-up mirrors, false eyelashes, hair spray, and curling irons. There were bras, tights, shoes, and glittery costumes lying all over the floor. Off in a corner with her back to the group was the director, sewing her pants. You would have never known she was present in the room, as she didn't engage with anyone at all.

A mom of an upperclassman who knew what was going on stepped into the doorway: "Girls, get your costumes on the rack: we're lining up soon." In the room, the chaos of hair and make-up continued. A few minutes later, she returned: "It's about time. Get your costumes on the rack." It was like no one ever entered the room and spoke. I looked around; not one single girl changed her behavior. I counted at least 12 costumes needed for their quick-change during the set still lying on the floor.

Girls continued to fix their faces. I looked over my shoulder to the director, who was still sitting with her back to the girls and doing nothing. This fueled my growing frustration. I felt it coming, rising up from my toes: my mom voice—that sharp, not-really-yelling but strong, assertive voice that makes everyone do a double-take.

"Girls! If your costume is not on that rack in 30 seconds, you will not compete. Get moving and line up!" I barked.

Heads spun and girls scampered to the costume rack. I looked to the corner where Rebecca and her best friend, Gwen, sat. Gwen looked at me with big eyes and a look of affirmation and said: "Mama Osgood, you get it." She and Rebecca gave each other a giggle and a smile. It stuck. Mama Osgood quickly became what the choir students called me. Even to those who didn't run in my kids' circles, I was Mama Osgood.

The Mysterious Artist

Apparently, Gwen and some of Rebecca's other friends were already calling me this in their own conversations, but it was that glorious, normal day at a show choir competition when a brick was laid in the foundation of my future. A stroke of paint was added to His canvas.

Enough of the foreshadowing. Let's spend a few chapters story-telling. God has a remarkable way of teaching me about His character. I never know what I'm learning until the lesson has passed. See if you can find the rainbows and the snowflakes.

Jesus replied, "You do not realize now what I am doing, but later you will understand."

John 13:7 (NIV)

Chapter 4
Self, Less

Then he said to them, "You like to appear righteous in public, but God knows your hearts."

Luke 16:15a

Are you familiar with a metronome? It is a device used by musicians to help them maintain a steady beat while they practice their music. A mechanical metronome is pyramid shaped and uses an adjustable weight on the end of an inverted pendulum rod to control tempo. The weight slides up the pendulum rod to decrease tempo or down to increase tempo. The pendulum swings back and forth, right to left, in tempo while a mechanism inside the metronome produces a clicking sound with each oscillation.

Like a metronome, I swung back and forth. On one side I was confident, trusting my abilities, and taking charge of my world. On the other side I was full of self-doubt, fear, and completely at a loss. Pretty regularly, I would tick back and forth, in and out of these opposing dispositions. Did that change when I had children? Uh, NO! Children moved the weight on the pendulum down and increased how quickly I would bounce between extremes.

To be honest, I'm not looking forward to talking with you about humility. First, the word is a derivative of humiliation. Who likes that feeling? And secondly, humility is not easily defined or quickly learned. Humility is far more than having manners and handling compliments. Humility is a heart issue.

Motherhood did something very important for me: it exposed my selfish nature. This was a severe mercy. I was at my ugliest from the time when the kids were infants and through preschool. They weren't good at playing independently, and I wasn't good at interactive play or being creative with our time. Days were like years filled with monotony; it seemed there were no signs of productivity or progress. Without trying, my wee little children held up a mirror that reflected who I really was. I didn't like what I saw. I was impatient, disconnected, and staring at the clock to see how much longer until Aaron got home from work. I thought my children misbehaved because they didn't like me, or because they wanted to get back at me for being a bad mom. Everything they did or didn't do, I took personally. I always made it about me. But God tapped me on the shoulder and said, *They're only children. They are just doing what they see you doing.* They were children; they didn't know better, but as an adult, I did. I had to start owning up to the condition of my heart.

Then came the season of sickness. God had to tear me down to construct something better. The five-month period I'm about to describe forced me to recognize both my selfishness and my helplessness. Rebecca was three and a half years old, and Jonathon was eighteen months, when we noticed a sudden, dramatic change in Rebecca's behavior. She was lethargic, mopey, and we'd even say depressed. *How can such a small child be depressed?*

In November she began vomiting (a lot) and for no apparent reason. During the day she would be hungry, but she did not want to eat. Sometimes she'd play, sometimes she'd throw up, but mostly she'd just lie around.

By mid-December the vomiting became like clockwork. It was the evenings and the nights when it all got ridiculous. After dinner, there would be some playtime with dad, a bath, and then she'd go off to bed. Within an hour or two of going to sleep, she'd throw up. Sometimes, it was just once. Other nights she would go to bed, throw up, go back to bed, throw up again, and so on. It was a good night if it only happened once, but there were other nights that we were washing her off in the bathtub repeatedly. Regardless, it happened every. single. night. I vividly remember one particular night when I was cleaning vomit out of her hair for the umpteenth time. It was an absurd hour, and Aaron was digging through the garage for an old sleeping bag, because we had made our way through all the extra bedding that we owned. Both Rebecca and I were crying, exhausted and desperate. All we seemed to know was washing vomit out of her hair in the bathtub in the middle of the night. No matter what I did, I couldn't help her, and I just wanted out. This is NOT what I envisioned when I thought of having a family.

We spent about three months working with specialists who tested her for many things, including celiac disease, ulcers, and food allergies, but everything came back inconclusive. Finally, thanks to internet research, I asked a specialist about H. pylori infection. They ran the test, and sure enough, that's what it was. H. pylori bacteria can be found in contaminated food or water. While we still don't know exactly how she got the bacteria, we believe that it likely came from our frequent camping trips that included a lot of lake swimming. We did this with her from the time she was a year old until her brother came along. The H. pylori bacteria likely lay dormant in her body for several months to a year. From November to March of her third year of life, we watched her mope through the day and vomit through the night, victim to H. pylori's sorcery. It took several rounds and many weeks of antibiotics before she returned to her spunky, sassy self.

Yes, that was horrible. But God used these things for my ultimate good. I needed to be really torn down before God could rebuild my life. In the middle of that season with Rebecca, Jonathon fought the rotavirus for three weeks. If you aren't familiar with rotavirus, it's a lovely ailment that leaves its victims vomiting and experiencing severe diarrhea. It was the dead of winter, my toddler daughter was vomiting day and night, and my infant son joined in adding the diarrhea. I can still remember coming out of the half bathroom with Rebecca who was dragging a vomit covered afghan behind her, only to find Jonathon crying in his highchair, the tray brimming with vomit, and sitting in a dirty diaper. You can imagine what my house smelled like for those three weeks. Rebecca was depressed and nauseated. Jonathon was fussy and covered with a severe diaper rash. I was broken-down, helpless, and just trying to survive. During this five-month season of sickness, I was floundering. I tried to believe more, trust

God more, and pray more. But my faith was small, my knowledge of God was even smaller, and my prayers were full of self-pity.

In May, the springtime brought fresh air, both my babies were healthy, and the house was sterilized and back to normal. After a winter of isolation, we were excited for our college friend to come to town for a visit. He had been living in Colorado for the last year. He was single, living large, and had an exciting business venture. During his visit, we spent the day chatting about his adventures and how Aaron's work was going. Finally, he intentionally looked at me and with genuine sincerity asked, "So Amy, what have you been doing?" My mind went utterly blank. All I could think about was the five months of nothing but vomiting and diarrhea, being shut out from the world with sick kids. Fighting back tears, all I could choke out was, "Laundry. I've been doing laundry."

I wasn't that great of a parent when the kids were small; some of that is just my wiring, I suppose. Once they were in school things got better. They had their activities and interests, and I had space to discover my own. When school days brought me a little freedom, our church connected me with a group who hosted a monthly lunch gathering of local organizations and ministry leaders to fellowship and to pray for the city. The first time I attended one of these meetings, I walked into a room of people whom I believed were world-changers. I felt insecure as I walked in alone, not knowing a single soul. Floating in my mind was, *Amy, what do you think you're doing here?* and *I don't have anything to offer.* When I walked in the door, I was greeted by a couple people who were several years younger than me. They were vibrant, confident, and talking with people they knew from work. I was immediately faced with, "Hi, Amy, what do you do?" As though I'd been punched, I had to clear my head to come up with some sort of answer: *Don't say "laundry." Don't say "laundry." Don't say "laundry."*

Let's not confuse humility with self-pity. I swam in the murky waters of self-pity—dwelling on one's own sorrows and misfortunes. Yes, I was happy to be a mom, and I loved my children to the ends of the earth. But my attention was on myself, focused on my lack of purpose and identity. I believed I had no value. At the heart of self-pity is pride. That is a mighty big pill to swallow. Read what C.S. Lewis has to say about pride in his book *Mere Christianity*[4].

> I pointed out a moment ago that the more pride one had, the more one disliked pride in others. In fact, if you want to find out how proud you are the easiest way is to ask yourself, 'How much do I dislike it when other people snub me, or refuse to take any notice of me, or shove their oar in, or patronize me, or show off?' The point is that each person's pride is in competition with everyone else's pride.

Well there you have it, friends. Pride. That was my problem. By definition, it still is whenever I get out of sorts. If I spend enough time and trace my feelings backwards, it usually comes back to believing my feelings have been hurt or believing I deserve better, etc. Beth Moore[5], Christian author and Bible teacher, paints the ugly but accurate truth about pride in her poem:

> My name is Pride.
> I am a cheater.
> I cheat you of your God-given destiny.
> I cheat you of contentment,
> Because you "deserve better than this."
> I cheat you of knowledge,
> Because you already know it all.
> I cheat you of healing,
> Because you're too full of me to forgive.
> I cheat you of holiness,
> Because you refuse to admit when you're wrong.
> I cheat you of vision,
> Because you'd rather look in the mirror than out a window.
> I cheat you of genuine friendship,

Because nobody's going to know the real you.
I cheat you of love,
Because real romance demands sacrifice.
I cheat you of greatness in heaven,
Because you refuse to wash another's feet on earth.
I cheat you of God's glory,
Because I convince you to seek your own.
My name is Pride.
I am a cheater.
You like me because you think I'm always looking out for you. Untrue.
I'm looking to make a fool of you.
God has so much for you, I admit,
But don't worry, if you stick with me, you'll never know.

Even though I felt very uncomfortable in the early days of attending the prayer group for the city, I continued to attend the monthly meetings for a few years. Eventually, I realized that these people didn't care what I did. It didn't matter if I was a director of a non-profit shelter, or pastor of a church, or a stay-at-home mom.

I came to pray, and that was all that mattered to them and to me. We were equal and valuable in the eyes of God.

Remember that metronome, where it swings from one extreme to the other? My favorite day of the week was Wednesday, because every Wednesday morning was women's Bible study. But this particular Wednesday, it was also the monthly city prayer meeting in the afternoon. Before running out the door like Homer Simpson yelling "Woohoo!", I tossed some laundry into the washing machine. The whole day was filled with sitting in God's Presence studying His Word with amazing women and then worshipping and praying with world-changers. I also had the opportunity to pray for a young woman I had just met who was battling migraines. We connected in a beautiful way. I love how God can make strangers feel like sisters in a matter of minutes. Driving home, I felt important, like I was a part of something bigger than myself. I didn't witness any miracles, no splitting of the sea, no manna from the sky, but it was special. I felt special.

As I pulled into the driveway at home, I remembered that there were wet clothes sitting in the washing machine. While I was bent over moving the clothes into the dryer, somewhere inside I felt like God said, *See, Amy, even on these great days of purpose and meaning, you still have to wash someone else's dirty underwear.* God would still speak to me through the laundry! He guarded my heart against self-pity *and* against self-elevation.

But there is another way beside the path of pride. Would you consider a few more definitions with me? Gospel-humility. Ever heard of it? I hadn't until I read Timothy Keller's booklet, called *The Freedom of Self-Forgetfulness*[6]. For the first time, I began to understand what it means to be humble, which has everything to do with the ego:

> The ego often hurts because it has something wrong with it…It is always making us think

about how we look and how we are treated. People sometimes say their *feelings* are hurt. But our *feelings* can't hurt. It is the *ego* that hurts – my sense of self, my identity.

If my ego is tender or wounded then my real struggle is my identity. The sooner I know who I am in God's eyes, the sooner I can break down the lies and behavior that I've used to protect my ego. When I operate in the love and acceptance of Christ, I am free to spend less time and energy on external affirmations and others' cues about how I'm doing. I can just be Amy rather than placing my value in how my children behave or in how they treat me.

Again, from Keller:

> Because the essence of gospel-humility is not thinking more of myself or thinking less of myself, it is thinking of myself, less. A truly gospel-humble person is not a self-hating

person or a self-loving person, but a gospel-humble person is a self-forgetful person.

What does it look like, as a mom, to think of myself less? It is not silently serving my family and fading into the upholstery. It is also not demanding and screaming that no one understands. Try on these two verses from the Bible. Somehow, we need to hold them the same way we hold two children at once, one on each hip.

1. Ephesians 2:10 *For we are God's masterpiece. He has created us anew in Christ Jesus, so we can do the good things he planned for us long ago.*

And

2. Isaiah 2:11a *Human pride will be brought down, and human arrogance will be humbled.*

You are God's masterpiece created in Christ Jesus to do good works. Lift that up, set it on your hip, and wrap your arm around it, pressing it close against you. Now, squat down and scoop up that we are full of pride: self-elevation and self-pity. Do a little lift-hop to situate that on your other hip, put your arm around it, and hold on. When we can walk into the world holding those two truths, like we were carrying our young children, the transformation can begin.

The remedy is simple. To overcome pride and our ego, we must find our identity in God. That is anything but easy. For me, finding my identity in Jesus took years—no, decades—of becoming self-aware and God-aware. I had to figure myself out, which is completely and utterly dangerous if I'm not discovering who God is as well. I could only come up with one personal example of gospel-humility. I am still working on this concept.

When Rebecca was in fourth grade, the teachers sponsored a big Sock Hop in the gym for the kids who completed their reading goals for the entire school year. Not wanting to miss an opportunity to dance and to see my daughter with her friends, I signed up to chaperone.

The elementary school's gym was darkened just enough to make one feel less exposed but not so dark that mischief could be hidden. The DJ lights were flashing, and the music was pumping out some seriously fun dance hits. I took my spot on the risers to watch the kids. My legs were tapping, and I was just itching to get out there and dance! I watched my daughter and her giggly pack, just standing there huddled together chatting. They'd move as a small herd to another spot in the gym, giggle, and chat some more. I sat there with a choice. Should I go to her group and start dancing, making every effort to be the fun, cool mom, and try to get them involved? Or, should I defer to her tender heart by leaving her to her friends and her own definition of fun? The wrong choice could have shattered her fragile, emerging self-image.

God provided my answer from a Bible study I was reading at the time as I watched her and her little tribe. John the Baptist said this of Jesus in John 3:30: "He must become greater and greater, and I must become less and less." I had been working on Jesus becoming greater and greater in my life. I then realized it was also the beginning of me becoming less and less to my kids, in order to make room for them to discover themselves. They didn't need to be in competition with me to see who was smarter, cooler, or funnier; they had that pressure everywhere else. My children have things to offer this world, and I needed to get out of their way, or they may have never discovered what they are called to, and what they are capable of accomplishing. I continue to learn humility—sometimes by their example.

A couple weeks before Jon was to graduate from high school, our community was unhinged by a school shooting in one of our middle schools. Praise God that there were no fatalities; however, a teacher and a student were significantly wounded. No one in our community will ever be the same. Each person in our town, and even in neighboring school districts, have their stories about that day. I can only tell the story of what happened in our home.

In the minutes following the shooting at the middle school, another threat was circulating, and the high school was put on lockdown. The high school students heard a rumor that the attack was part of a three-pronged plan and that the other middle school and high school were next. This rumor was untrue. Regardless, terror was thick in the darkened school while students were barricaded in their silent classrooms for more than 90 minutes. They could hear first responder's footsteps in the halls, weapons rattling in their hands, as they knocked on doors. For many students, they could not tell if those sounds were people keeping them safe, or if it was another gunman about to kick in their classroom door. Confusion and fear held everyone captive.

My husband and I followed the news, and, after not hearing from Jon, we sent him a text. He simply replied with which classroom he was in, and that he was OK. After several hours, the threat was proven benign, and students were to be slowly released from the building. This took up nearly the entire school day. Finally, Jon walked in the door, glanced at the TV, and quietly asked if we could turn off the news coverage. He was shell-shocked and really didn't have much that he felt like sharing. I don't think he knew where to begin. He had already scheduled to meet with his mentor from church, and we told him to go ahead and go. It would be good to process with someone outside our school community. Cyrus would be a good listener.

While Jon was in his meeting, I got a call from the father of one of Jon's friends. The dad identified himself and proceeded to thank Aaron and me for the kind of son we had raised. I was absolutely confused. I didn't know what on earth he was talking about. Sensing my confusion, he said, "I assumed Jon told you what happened in class." He continued, "Lauryn was scared to death today and could not pull herself together. She was panicking. Jon sat on the floor with her for hours. He held her hand and told her he'd take care of her. He'd make sure if they had to run for their lives, she could run with him to his car, and they'd look for her boyfriend, together. He assured her he wouldn't leave her side." Her dad continued, "You know, a couple days ago at the school banquet, I asked Jon to keep an eye on Lauryn at college." "Jon answered, 'You bet I will!' Amy, Jon was true to his word already. Please thank him for us."

I hung up the phone, and I burst into tears as I tried to explain what happened to Aaron. A couple hours later, Jon got home. We said, "Lauryn's dad called." Jon's face fell as he was afraid that he did something wrong.

"Jon, why didn't you tell us how you took care of Lauryn today?"

With the sincerest heart he said, "Mom, she was *really* upset. I didn't think she'd want me telling other people."

That is thinking of self, less. Humility.

We all have a tendency to bounce from one extreme to the other like a metronome. But when a living, intentional relationship with God is a part of my life, the fear and insecurity is calmed, and my confidence and control is rooted in God's character, not mine. As life ticks on, day in and day out, God is bringing all things into balance. And on my best days, I put that metronome into the locked position like the Apostle Paul suggests in 1 Corinthians 4:3-5 (NIV):

I care very little if I am judged by you or by any human court; indeed, I do not even judge myself. My conscience is clear, but that does not make me innocent. It is the Lord who judges me. Therefore judge nothing before the appointed time; wait until the Lord comes. He will bring to light what is hidden in darkness and will expose the motives of the heart. At that time each will receive their praise from God.

Chapter 5
Freedom

And he said, "Yes, it was written long ago that the Messiah would suffer and die and rise from the dead on the third day. It was also written that this message would be proclaimed in the authority of his name to all the nations, beginning in Jerusalem: 'There is forgiveness of sins for all who repent.'"

Luke 24:46-47

Rarely do I get the opportunity to brag about myself, mostly because I'm short on material. But one day, long ago, I had a brilliant moment. When people ask me how my kids became such close friends, I go back to this story.

The kids weren't quite school-aged yet, maybe kindergarten and preschool. Regardless, it was summertime. The days were long, and the words "I'm bored" flowed freely from the lips of my spawn. We had just moved into a new neighborhood, so we didn't know anyone yet. No neighbor kids to send them outside to play with. They were bored and enjoyed making a game of getting on each other's nerves, not to mention mine.

Jonathon would poke at his sister and run away; then, he would sweetly return and offer suggestions of things they could do. Rebecca tried to ignore him. If she acknowledged him, it was only to reject every idea he had. There was some fun for her in turning him down. The kids were dancing but not to music. They swayed in and out of meanness, taunting, and rejection. After the hundredth time of "Mom, she's...," and "Mom, he's...," finger-pointing, and blame, blame, blame, I did the ultimate upside-down. On a normal day, I would have separated the two, each to their own bedroom. You know what usually happens? They would continue to taunt each other through their bedroom walls. Then, they would yell to me that they were sorry and were ready to get out, when really, they had just come up with a new way to provoke the other, and they were ready to try it out. But this time I played a mom card that they didn't know I had.

In total exasperation and with great resolve, I said, "Sit down, right here, the both of you." We had a small step that connected the kitchen to the sunken family room. This step was smack in the middle of everything. They were completely in my sight. I did not remove myself from their presence, and I did not separate them. They had to sit next to each other on that step. Then, I did the worst thing I could do in their eyes.

"Now, hold hands."

Shock and terror crossed their little faces.

"I don't like her."

"He's so annoying."

"Yes, but hold hands."

In the mind of a child, seconds are like months, and minutes are like years, but this became a glorious moment. At the beginning of Mama's new time-out, they were as still as statues, angry, and trying to hide their feelings from me. They didn't think I could see, but they were silently squeezing all circulation out of each other's hand. Then something happened. An invisible switch flipped. Jonathon moved a finger, and it tickled. We are not sure if the finger movement was an involuntary reflex, a small cry for blood flow, or if he intentionally moved his finger in an attempt to get Rebecca into trouble. Rebecca, not wanting to relent in her scorn for her brother or to show any loss of resolve, still couldn't help but smirk at the tickle. That's all it took for Jonathon. This one tiny tickle kicked off a new game. Who could make the other smirk? Who could one-up the other and make him smile? Finally, who could make the other laugh? Surely, they would get into more trouble for laughing during time-out. Seriously, within a couple minutes, my two mini enemies were laughing together on that small step between the kitchen and family room. Trying to make the other smile ended up being pretty fun!

Forgiveness never feels as simple as a little game of holding hands on the step. If someone hurt me, the last thing I'd want to do is make them smile. Someone hurt me, treated me unjustly, called me names, or didn't do what I wanted them to do. By being mad, and staying mad, I could justify myself. Keeping the pain of their wound alive justified my feelings. Often, when I did go to God in prayer over the circumstance or the person, I usually prayed, *God he's so…* and *God, I can't believe she'd…* Finger-pointing and blame just seems a whole lot easier; besides, I'm right—right?

Like in the chapter on humility, a few definitions will prove helpful. Here are a few powerful truths about forgiveness that I learned from my Christian counselor. I later discovered these same nuggets of wisdom in an article in *Greater Good Magazine*[7].

Forgiveness is *for you*, not for the one you are forgiving.

> …forgiveness brings the *forgiver* peace of mind and frees him or her from corrosive anger. While there is some debate over whether true forgiveness requires positive feelings toward the offender, experts agree that it at least involves letting go of deeply held negative

feelings. In that way, it empowers you to recognize the pain you suffered without letting that pain define you, enabling you to heal and move on with your life. [Emphasis mine]

If you forgive those who sin against you, your heavenly Father will forgive you. But if you refuse to forgive others, your Father will not forgive your sins.

Matthew 6:14-15

Up to this point on my journey with forgiveness, I believed that if I forgave someone it was really to help them out. I felt like a queen who forgave my silly maidservant for not doing what I wanted, like I had some authority over her. Forgiveness isn't about authority. Forgiveness is about my freedom, not the person I'm forgiving. My peace of mind and energy are at stake. Forgiveness validates my feelings but doesn't trap me in pain and negative emotions.

The article in *Greater Good Magazine* continues their definition. Forgiveness is a decision not a feeling.

Psychologists generally define forgiveness as a conscious, *deliberate decision* to release feelings of resentment or vengeance toward a person or group who has harmed you, regardless of whether they actually deserve your forgiveness. Just as important as defining what forgiveness *is*, though, is understanding what forgiveness is *not*. Experts who study or teach forgiveness make clear that when you forgive, you do not gloss over or deny the seriousness of an offense against you. Forgiveness does not mean forgetting, nor does it mean condoning or excusing offenses. Though forgiveness can help repair a damaged relationship, it doesn't obligate you to reconcile with the person who harmed you, or release them from legal accountability. [Emphasis mine]

For this is how God loved the world: He gave his one and only Son, so that everyone who believes in him will not perish but have eternal life. God sent his Son into the world not to judge the world, but to save the world through him.

John 3:16-17

Jesus chose. He decided to sacrifice Himself, even though he did nothing wrong. It is a choice to let go. No one really feels like letting go. It's scary, and it simply doesn't feel right or safe. It is a risk. Forgiveness does not initially feel good. Nonetheless, when I choose to let go, to give up resentment, I am the one set free.

And now for the big one:

Forgiveness is NEVER, EVER earned.

If forgiveness could be earned, there would be no need for it. We might live out our consequences because of our wrongdoing, but that doesn't mean we have earned forgiveness. It has always been, and always will be, a gift. Those who hurt us don't deserve forgiveness, and we ourselves don't deserve forgiveness when we mess up. Wrong is wrong.

We are made right with God by placing our faith in Jesus Christ. And this is true for everyone who believes, no matter who we are. For everyone has sinned; we all fall short of God's glorious standard. Yet God, in his grace, freely makes us right in his sight. He did this through Christ Jesus when he freed us from the penalty for our sins.

Romans 3:22-24

My husband and I are friends with a newly married couple. Sadly, after a year or so of marriage, this new husband had a lapse in judgment and a moment of infidelity. The couple chose to do the hard work of forgiveness, redemption, and rebuilding trust. Aaron and I sat at their small table in their apartment and listened. The young wife told us the recent instruction she received from the pastor that married them: "Only God can forgive, all we can do is say, 'I'm forgiving.'" This instantly reminded me of the scene from the movie *The Shack* where Mac, the father, was carrying his daughter's abused and murdered little body. With each step, he whispered through tears, "I forgive." "I forgive." "I forgive." Forgiveness is a painful, difficult decision.

Understanding that forgiveness is a decision, not a feeling, helped me, but it wasn't enough. When I discovered that forgiveness is actually spiritual warfare, that made it a game-changer. Allow to me to try and explain. Since Jesus defeated sin on the Cross by His unmerited punishment, He defeated the enemy:

> *"He canceled the record of the charges against us and took it away by nailing it to the cross. In this way, he disarmed the spiritual rulers and authorities. He shamed them publicly by his victory over them on the cross."*
>
> Colossians 2:14-15

Jesus disarmed the enemy with the forgiveness of my sins. Therefore, I defeat the enemy when I forgive others who sin against me. I no longer live under that pain and burden. The enemy is silenced when I forgive, and I can no longer cling to what he wants me to hang onto. By forgiving, I take away the enemy's weapon.

All this new knowledge about forgiveness was a great foundation, but I needed a lot of courage to walk through the door of forgiveness myself. God has an uncanny pattern of teaching me something and then giving me an opportunity to practice what I learned. Just knowing the truth about forgiveness would not set me free. It was actually in the forgiving that I found freedom.

Sometime in my early thirties, I was reading *Breaking the Enemy's Grip*[8] by Eddie and Alice Smith. This book addressed generational sin and brokenness. There were several exercises in prayer, one of which included making a list of sins. To claim victory, I had to acknowledge where I had gone wrong. Not only that, but the authors encouraged the list to contain the sins of my family as well, at least the ones I was aware of. It was confession on steroids. People today do body cleanses all the time to reset the body: a digestive cleanse, a skin cleanse, and so on. If you have ever done one, you know how difficult and uncomfortable it is. It's a shock to the system. It's counter-intuitive. It doesn't "feel" good or right. What I was about to do was a soul cleanse.

I wrote on several pieces of paper every sin that I had committed or that my birth family had committed. It took more sheets of paper than I'd like to admit. But I called it what it was. Sin. No excuses. Per the instructions in the book, I read the sins aloud and asked for forgiveness. When I got through all those pages, then, as an indicator that the sins were gone, I set the sheets of paper on fire. No evidence of our mistakes. This process was powerful and helpful. But through this exercise, I realized something hidden deep in my heart. I had unresolved unforgiveness specifically towards my mom. I was absolutely shocked when God showed me this. I had no idea that that was at the root of my inability to live in freedom.

My mom was, and is, a great mom. She worked hard, and I know her attention was divided among many interests and demands. Add to that, I was very much an unexpected pregnancy and birth. Deep inside I believed that I was unwanted and an inconvenience to my family. This wasn't true, but no one could convince me otherwise. As a child I had a lot of emotional needs, and no human could have ever met those needs. But I looked to my mom to fill them—all of them. I was never angry at her, and I loved her dearly. I knew she didn't always get it right, but I also knew she was doing the best she could. Once I became a mom with school-aged children, my appreciation and understanding of my own mom only grew and grew. So, when God revealed unforgiveness in me, I was shocked. I had no idea this plagued my soul. I also didn't know what I was missing on the other side of forgiveness.

The day of freedom came shortly after finishing reading the book and burning those pages. The kids were on the bus to school, and my husband was out the door to work. No one was home. I took this time to pray about the revealed feelings I had toward mom. In just moments I collapsed in grief with the weight of the unforgiveness that I was carrying. Instead of just glossing over my emotions and saying, *I forgive her*, I began to tell God how hurt I was. I couldn't forgive her until I got all my feelings out. I didn't say mean things about her, I was just honest about how I felt. Then the sweet, choking words came out—all by themselves. *I forgive Mom for_____. I forgive Mom for_____. I forgive her for_____. And I forgive Mom for not being able to meet all my needs.*

To say I was crying is an understatement; 30-some years of held emotions flowed across my face. I'm sure there were real mistakes she made; however, I am also sure I remembered circumstances that may have not been true or accurate. Regardless, acknowledging my feelings, both real and perceived, was powerful. By the work of God, the waterfalls from my eyes slowly subsided, and without effort or thought, I found myself laughing. I was overwhelmed with such a lightness and freedom! I sat on the kitchen floor in relief and joy. I was practically giggling which revealed an unspeakable peace. Only God can turn our tears to laughter in such an inexplicable way. I knew then that I had really let it go. The blinders of pain were off, and I saw my mom through new, clear eyes. My vision of her now was of indescribable love. Interestingly, my mom was never involved in the transaction. It was completely between me and God.

We don't always get tidy endings. Most of the time, we have to continue in faith that forgiveness has happened, and that something new is blooming. But this time, God put some icing on the cake. About a year later after that beautiful day on my kitchen floor, my family and I were on a long drive with my parents. The men were in the front, my mom and I sat side by side in the middle section, and the kids in the back of the van. Mom leaned over and said, "God's been working on me, and He made me realize something. I never thanked Him for the gift He gave me thirty-five years ago." I was thirty-five years old at the time, and I knew exactly what she meant. Because of the transaction on my kitchen floor a year prior, I could recognize the vulnerable courage it took Mom to say she never thanked God for me. My heart was instantly flooded. The beauty was, I was able to accept her comment. I was free to receive it. I didn't judge, fearing there could be an ulterior motive. I wasn't busy self-protecting. I had nothing blocking the love she was sending to me. Now, when she and I talk about the way things were while I was growing up, I am so grateful for all that did, and all that did not, happen in my childhood. Every piece of it led me to God. Every joy from my childhood is even deeper, and every hurt is cleansed, healed, and rendered powerless, stamped with God's love. There truly is so much freedom in forgiveness.

But God didn't stop there! Next, I would be the mom in need of forgiveness. My daughter was in middle school, and she was experiencing tremendous amounts of anxiety. Details will be elusive here because it is her story to tell, should she ever want to tell it. But her anxiety was deep, and there were visible signs of her distress. In all my parenting efforts, I knew that I was doing my best to help her find peace and get well. But God again revealed something I didn't know about myself: *Amy, you're part of the problem.* At her tender age and in her emotional state, I could never ask her *IF* I was part of the problem. She would have said "no" out of fear of rocking a fragile boat. I had no business putting pressure on her to choose between herself and her loyalty to me. If my mom would have asked me if she was missing the mark, I would have defended her and said, "No, Mom, I'm fine." But God showed me my error, so I didn't need Rebecca to tell me I was part of the problem. I knew I was, and I knew what I had to do. One afternoon I said to her, "I know there are things you have needed from me, and I'm sorry I didn't take care of you the way I should have. You needed me to do something, and I didn't. I have not given you what you've needed. I am so sorry."

For some reason, we fantasize what reconciliation should look like. We think we say we're sorry and everything will immediately be better. This, however, almost never happens. It takes time for people to process, feel, and accept. Forgiveness could mean several conversations, not just an apology and off you go. Remember, God spent a year working on my mom after I forgave her in the privacy of my home. This particular day with Rebecca was no different. I sincerely apologized to her, and she knew it. Regardless, she didn't say anything back to me. She may have nodded slightly, but she walked out of the room. It never came up again. Again, I had to believe, in faith, that something unseen settled between us. God asked me to trust Him that forgiveness had happened, and maybe there was room for something new—something better—to grow.

You can't have a chapter on forgiveness and not have confessions. Here are my top three on the subject, in no particular order:

- I have moments when I ask for forgiveness only to get results. That's not forgiveness; that's manipulation.
- I also sometimes say, "I'm sorry but…" Hmm, I'm probably not "really" sorry then. I'm trying to excuse myself.
- I want to avoid feeling bad, so I take shortcuts.

In all these cases, internal work needs to be done. My freedom and joy are at stake. It is in my best interest to let God dig around in my heart and mind. It is good for me to wrestle with Him and my true feelings and motives.

When forgiveness has been necessary in my life, Jesus doesn't banish me to my room, like I usually did with my children. He knew I would continue to stew in my hurt and plot what I would do when my "time-out" was over. Instead, He stayed present with me in the middle of everything, just like my kids on the step. Figuratively, He asked me to sit with my mom, and then my daughter, and hold their hands.

Forgiveness is a journey. Even when someone does the unthinkable, forgiveness is there, waiting in the wings for me to embrace it. Just this week, I have had to work through forgiving precious, silly, stubborn people in my life who have hurt me. In fact, when my adult children are back home for the summer, I am in need of their forgiveness as I try to figure out how to parent "children" who are in charge of their own lives. Whether I'm forgiving someone, forgiving myself, or in need of being forgiven, it always brings freedom.

Oh, what joy for those whose disobedience is forgiven, whose sin is put out of sight! Yes, what joy for those whose record the LORD has cleared of guilt, whose lives are lived in complete honesty! When I refused to confess my sin, my body wasted away, and I groaned all day long. Day and night your hand of discipline was heavy on me. My strength evaporated like water in the summer heat. Finally, I confessed all my sins to you and stopped trying to hide my guilt. I said to myself, "I will confess my rebellion to the LORD." And you forgave me! All my guilt is gone.

Psalm 32:1-5

Chapter 6

Leaning In

Once Jesus was in a certain place praying. As he finished, one of his disciples came to him and said, "Lord, teach us to pray, just as John taught his disciples."

Luke 11:1

When was the last time someone told you a secret? There's something special and intimate about someone sharing a secret. You lean in, put your ear close enough to their mouth to feel their breath whisper across your skin, hold perfectly still, and focus intently on what they are about to say. Maybe the last time you felt that brush of breath across your ear was because you were in a crowded, noisy room, and someone was trying to make sure you heard them. The idea of leaning in best describes the posture of prayer for me.

More than any other chapter, I wish we were across the table from each other talking about this face to face. I'd rather hear about your experiences and learn from you.

Leaning In

I am no expert, just a fellow journeyman. Prayer is too big a subject to conquer in just a few pages. So, I'm not going to. Instead, I'd like to take us to the One with whom we are communicating. Just googling "prayer" for a definition points to the fact that prayer is to God or an object of worship. This begs the question, who am I worshipping?

If prayer is communicating with an object of worship (pretty rudimentary definition), then the following questions need to be asked:

- Is my object of worship something or someone that will communicate in response to me?
- Is there give and take—talking and listening?
- Do I make any effort to communicate?
- Do I listen?

Before you slam this book shut because these are really difficult questions to answer, let me assure you this discipline of prayer is still evolving for me personally, and it is full of ups and downs. I'm messy and still trying to figure it out. My prayer life can be as disorienting as standing in a tornado or as empty as sitting in a dark cave. Hop on the roller coaster of prayer with me…

My earliest experience with prayer was completely done out of obedience, making sure I said what I was supposed to say. It was a lot more like reciting a poem or a creed. If you were to hear my prayers then, they would have reflected my belief in the existence of a God, but that He would only protect me and take care of me if I said the words correctly and if I said them every day. As I got older my prayers changed. I was disconnected from my so-called object of worship. Therefore, my prayers were more like to-do lists or wish lists for a genie in a bottle. What brought about this change?

When the kids were toddlers, I completed my first women's Bible study. I asked my small group leader what she was going to study for the next session, as we could choose between three different courses. Her response poked at an empty area of my heart in need of being filled. She said, "I'm going to study *Lord I Want to*

Know You by Kay Arthur. I figured I should know just exactly Who it is I'm praying to." Even though my attitudes, patterns, and motives have bounced all over the place, this one truth remains: prayer is always about leaning in and getting to know God better.

When my little Rebecca was a toddler, and Jonathon was even smaller, we were driving home one day. The kids were strapped in their car seats behind me. Rebecca was gazing out the window softly and sweetly singing, "Jesus Loves Me" when Jonathon started to talk to her, or rather talk at her. She immediately stopped her delightful song, swung her head around as though swinging a punch and screamed at him with venom, "STOP IT!! I'M SINGING TO JESUS!!" she then instantly returned to the sweet tones as she looked back out her car window.

Rebecca's contradictory tones are like the ebb and flow of my prayer life. I would say one thing, almost believing I meant it, only to get up from praying and go on with my deep-seated biases, agendas, and attitudes.

I have treated God like a genie in a bottle expecting Him to do as I say. Or I ask, and ask, and ask, and ask, and never exercise any faith.

Want some proof? I'll show you what I mean.

While Rebecca was in first grade, our family doctor said, "I want to send her to an otolaryngologist." That's just a really hard word to pronounce for an ear, nose, and throat doctor. Rebecca's ears worked perfectly, but they protruded significantly from her sweet face. Our family doctor and the otolaryngologist worked together to quickly make arrangements. The appointment was scheduled, and before I knew it, we were talking about plastic surgery on my six-year-old baby!

I am usually a decisive person but this one had me unglued. Yes, clearly, I could see that her ears protruded. My husband and I were sure she would spend her young life being teased and feeling self-conscious because of her ears. But, I did NOT want to instill in my young daughter that if you don't like something about yourself, you get surgery, or that you should focus on outer beauty rather than inner beauty. That is simply a value we do not hold.

Since I was beside myself with worry and scared to death of making the wrong decision for her, I tried to fast and pray. This was the first time for me. So, I warned God I wasn't going to eat the next day. This is how that prayer conversation went—as though He didn't already know—*Tomorrow, God, I'm going to fast. If You can tell me a way to explain to Rebecca that she's beautiful just the way she is—but we might have her get surgery to fix her ears—then I'll move forward and go to the appointment with the ear surgeon.* Yes, I totally bargained with God: "if You, then I."

Before I went to bed that night, I told my prayer and fasting plan to Aaron. But my explanation quickly turned into an overexaggerated rant.

"What if she thinks there's something wrong with her?"

"What if she puts too much emphasis on her appearance because of the trend we could be starting?"

"What if she thinks we don't like the way she looks?"

"What if she struggles to meet friends because kids are mean?"

"If she asks, 'why am I having surgery?' what on earth are we going to tell her?"

Then the LORD shut me up with Aaron's perfect response to my rhetoric:

"Amy, we just tell her that we're going to fix her ears so they don't get in the way."

It was that simple. It was true. I was flooded with peace.

Even though God answered me *before* I fasted, I decided to go ahead with the plan anyway. I figured I should keep my word to God. Just so you know, I'm a terrible "faster," always have been, probably always will be. I have friends who love to fast. They feel so close to God when they do. Yeah, that's not me. I usually realize how much I love my comfort, and I end up feeling pretty rotten about what fasting reveals about my selfish, indulgent nature. But I think my perfect Heavenly Father was delighted that I tried, like when a baby begins to walk, all wobbly and awkward. I think that's how God felt about me that day. I like to think He giggled with parental pride as He watched me try. Regardless, nothing magical happened when my fast was over the next day.

Aaron and I agreed to move forward. Rebecca had her otoplasty ear surgery over Christmas break of her first grade year. A couple weeks before the surgery, we had our final consultation with the doctor. Rebecca and I were in the waiting room when a man came out from the offices to check the large aquarium that sat in the middle of the room. He was apparently the Medical Administrator for the whole practice.

"Rebecca Osgood, we're ready for you," called the nurse.
The man turned to us and said, "Rebecca? I'm Sarah's dad from your class!"

Sarah was Rebecca's best friend at the time; they had just met a few months before. I smiled and thanked God for the sweet hint to keep moving forward. I suppose I could have read that "sign" in many different ways. Nonetheless, I was comforted by a friendly face and thanked God for it.

Later that day as I was fixing dinner, the phone rang. It was Sarah's dad. He said that Rebecca had been a really special friend to Sarah. Sarah was an only child, so her friends were very important to her. Then he said, "I see Rebecca is having both of her ears pinned so they sit closer to her head. I talked with your doctor, and we both agreed that we are only going to charge you for one ear. We are giving you a 50% discount."

I stayed cool on the phone, but as soon as we hung up, I fell to the floor in tears. God blessed my intentions to do what was best and to pursue Him through the whole process.

Remember me saying that prayer is a journey? Just because I made it through one part, doesn't mean I continued to walk in faith through the rest of the process. Even though God showed me He was in this, I didn't walk into the surgery with the confidence of Christ. One might think that since God was so clear and gracious leading up to this point, I would have been full of faith. Nope! I was right back to replaying my fears: *What if there is irreversible damage? What if she doesn't wake up from the anesthesia?* Even after God's evident hand, I still lay at the foot of her bed and wept the night before the surgery, begging God not to take her from me. Because I was so scared, I thought I could manipulate God by fasting again. I tried to prove to God that He should take care of her because I was going to fast the day of the surgery.

The next morning, I sat in the waiting room, stomach growling, with an open book in my lap. In an effort to look busy and not reveal my eyes brimming with tears, I pretended to read. I never turned a page…for 90 minutes. Not one page. I did, however, look at my watch—frequently. Every time medical staff came from the hall, I anticipated the dreaded pronouncement:

"Mrs. Osgood, we have bad news: she didn't make it through the surgery."

Well, eventually, a nurse did come out and told us that everything had gone perfectly! We made our way back to post-op where Rebecca was waking up. She had two ponytails sitting high and tight on her scalp, sticking out of the tan ACE bandages that ringed her head. I took one look at her…and passed out. Boom! A nurse grabbed me, plopped me in a chair, and reached for the smelling salt. I had prayed and fasted, but neither had guaranteed that Rebecca or I would sail through the surgery.

My rural childhood provided many opportunities to watch the graceful descent of water birds naturally and instinctively moving from flight to float. While I thought I could be that soaring prayer person who exercises faith and trust at the same time, I wasn't. I didn't soar through Rebecca's ear surgery, trusting God because He is faithful. I looked more like a wounded duck shot out of the sky trying to find a pond only to crash on the shore.

Fast forward thirteen years. Maybe this time with Jon, I'll get it right. Place your bets. Was I obedient? Did I have faith? Did God come through for me?

During Jon's senior year of high school, he began to audition for college musical theatre programs. The audition process was grueling. There was a lot of information to track, and if a deadline was missed, there was no grace. Two weeks before his first in-person college audition, I was frantic. Jon was in the middle of rehearsals for his part in the high school musical, so I was managing all the auditioning details.

One particular day was planned full during his fall break. First was his voice lesson. After that, we were off to record his video audition for the prescreening process, which was required by some of the universities. Jon woke up that morning with what appeared to be pink eye. Full of faith and confidence, I went to my room to pray. *Unexpected illness is not too hard for God*, I mused. I asked God to heal Jon, knowing full well that He is able. I also knew these deadlines were a big deal, and Jon needed every opportunity to get into the school that would be best for him. But what I thought was confidence in Christ turned out to be selfish arrogance.

To tell the truth, I had a plan, and we had things to do that day, and that was my heart. We pressed on. I picked up Jon's accompanist, and we drove to his voice lesson while Jon's condition worsened by the minute. He was bent over in the backseat with his eyes closed because they hurt so bad. With his voice coach, Jon sang through his material for an hour in an ultra-dark room just so he could keep his eyes open. He wiped the tears and drainage from his eyes throughout the entire lesson. I relented on the video audition because he looked absolutely horrible! He struggled to hold his infected eyes open, as a powerful headache came on. You have full permission to judge me for being a tyrant and for being completely insensitive to how Jon was feeling. I deserve it.

His condition deteriorated rapidly. By that afternoon, we called to get an emergency appointment with an ophthalmologist who could diagnose what was happening. By now God had humbled me, revealing to me my attitude and my behavior. That morning I had been confident that Jon would be healed; by that afternoon I sat in the waiting room for an emergency appointment, texting friends and pastors for prayer. Jon had lost vision—which continued for two days—and struggled through excruciating eye pressure. I was scared for Jon. I was also terribly ashamed that I had treated God like a genie. I had expected God to get on board with my plans and my timetable.

Jon lived for five days in painful darkness before he showed signs of any improvement. We returned to the ophthalmologist for the next three months for multiple follow up appointments. Even though Jon's sight returned, he continued to have high levels of eye pressure and unknown flakes in his cornea that needed treatment. At our very last visit the doctor said, "I've never seen viral conjunctivitis do this before. Truly, I have never had a case like this. But, good news, he is finally fully cleared."

Praise God, Jon had no permanent damage, just terrible memories. Me? I now know not to confuse that just because God COULD heal my son, for my convenience, it doesn't mean that He SHOULD.

Could there be more to praying than just getting what we want? What if God brings people and circumstances along my path so I will pray, not for me, but for someone else? With God, there is always more beneath the surface.

When Rebecca was in second grade, she befriended a little girl who was not the type of person she was usually drawn to. I watched this little girl's behavior, and I was convinced she was not a good friend for Rebecca. The first thing that came to my mind was Rebecca's safety. Responding to my own wishes, I prayed that this friendship would end. There was nothing wrong with being concerned for Rebecca's safety, but there was something else that was more important to God. I have learned that if I set God's agenda first, He always brings my kids through.

Anyway, we had a rule in our house that either Aaron or I had to meet or talk to the parents before any playdates would be allowed. I had a phone call with this little girl's mom, and I quickly decided that any playdates would be at my house. When I hung up the phone, it occurred to me that this had nothing to do with Rebecca. It had everything to do with her little friend. She needed to be prayed for. Maybe that was why she entered our world. With a fresh perspective, I began faithfully praying for this little girl. God only knows, I may have been the only person on the face of the earth to lift her name up before the King of Kings. Rebecca's second grade friendship—that was nonexistent by third grade—radically changed my perspective going forward. When friends or boyfriends or girlfriends or teachers entered our world, they were always covered in prayer. It wasn't my job to manipulate my kids' friendships and relationships. My job was to pray for the people God brought into our lives. The nature of the relationships usually worked themselves out on their own.

This led me to believe that God wasn't just bringing people into our lives who needed prayer. Maybe He was strategically placing me in volunteer roles in the classroom, dance company, or choir program for a greater purpose. Could this be my ministry? Agent Osgood, Undercover Prayer Warrior! In subsequent chapters, you will see why God placed this in my heart. A season of desperate prayer was coming.

But if I was going to be praying for people out of my grasp but in my life, or praying for situations far greater than myself, I was going to need some tools. Scripture, along with praise and worship music, were keys that unlocked a whole new world. The more I knew God, the more I could recognize Him. When I saw Him working, it inspired me to trust Him with bigger things. Both the Word and music provided language when I was at a loss for words. Let's start with the Word of God.

By the time Rebecca was in second grade and Jonathon was in kindergarten, God had blessed me with a group of women, each of us in various life stages. There were six of us, the oldest of which was 40 years older than me, and the rest were 10-15 years older. I was the baby in the group and these older women of deep faith—true prayer warriors—were raising me.

With both kids in school, I asked God "What's next?" I had more day time available, and I was sure He had more important stuff for me to do. One of the women from this precious group asked me which elementary school my kids attended. By no accident, that school needed a leader for Moms In Prayer (MIP). MIP is an international ministry that prays for schools (but not in the schools). Moms of school-aged children gather once a week for one hour to pray. MIP has no affiliation with any specific denomination or with the school itself. The school was simply how the moms were connected.

Moms in Prayer also has a strict format to follow, completely grounded in Scripture. This strict format ensured we would finish in one hour, and it kept us focused on God's Word and His character. Nowadays, MIP has the weekly prayer sheet resource available on their website, but back in my day, I had to prepare the prayer sheet each and every week. This had me thumbing through the Bible…a lot. I was amazed that Scripture said everything that needed to be said. This experience showed me a much better way to pray, especially when I couldn't create the words to say on my own. I still remember the first verse I prayed with my kids' names in it: "I pray that the eyes of (Rebecca and Jonathon's) heart may be enlightened in order that they may know the hope to which He has called them, the riches of His glorious inheritance in His holy people, and His incomparably great power for us who believe." (Ephesians 1:18-19a NIV) Though I don't understand all of Scripture, it became clear that the Word reliably taught me about God, and it gave me words to pray for my kids. Plus, I could be encouraged because God's Word accomplishes what IT is supposed to:

As the rain and the snow come down from heaven, and do not return to it without watering the earth and making it bud and flourish, so that it yields seed for the sower and bread for the eater, so is my word that goes out from my mouth: It will not return to me empty, but will accomplish what I desire and achieve the purpose for which I sent it.

Isaiah 55:10-11 NIV

Declaring God's promises over my kids was such a reassurance. I didn't have to understand everything; I just had to pray. Truly, His Word has been my greatest prayer tool! I discovered the Psalms when I did not have the words to express my grief, my pain, and my doubt. There were also New Testament promises to cling to. The books of Ephesians, Philippians, and Colossians are personal favorites. When I became fearful, I reminded myself time and time again of Who really was in control. I would declare over and over:

...I am not ashamed for I know the One in whom I trust, and I am sure that he is able to guard (Rebecca and Jonathon) what (whom) I have entrusted to him until the day of his return.

2 Timothy 1:12

In the same way Moms In Prayer opened me up to praying Scripture, praise and worship music made it easy to express what I could not. This would happen at our weekly church services, but I quickly got CDs (remember those?), and I found radio stations to redirect my thinking through worship. When my heart was heavy over someone (usually my kids), musical worship often said what I wanted to say or needed to say when I simply couldn't. Sometimes the songs would remind me that God knows, cares, and is working on their behalf. I can't sing—not in a way that anyone would want to listen—but singing praise and worship songs taught me to rehearse God's truth. It would do everything from reassure me, to convict me, to give me the words to pray over the things that concerned my heart.

God invited me to bring even the little things in my life to Him during my praise and worship time. During Rebecca's sophomore year of high school, her show choir hired a new Associate Director. He may not have been the overall director, but he was assigned to the varsity women's show choir. This man was young, talented, and appeared to care about the girls. He worked hard to draw out their talent and rebuild the success they missed their freshman year. Within her sophomore school year alone, the varsity women's choir had unprecedented success as they placed high at competitions. The girls had a miracle goal: to make it to Show Choir State Finals. On the last Saturday to qualify for the state competition, the group did not advance to the finals, and it seemed like their season was over. There were a lot of tears on that bus ride home. The girls knew they were good and that they had improved so much; disappointment ran deep.

The next morning at church, one of the worship songs was "Turn it Around" by Israel & New Breed. I couldn't help but ask God to turn around what appeared to be the end of an amazing show choir season. I didn't know how it could happen, but the lyrics of "Turn It Around" inspired me to ask, "Turn it around/open the windows of Heaven, pour out a blessing overflow/turn it around/open the windows of Heaven, pour out a blessing we cannot contain/let it rain."

That same Sunday afternoon, texts were blowing up all over the girls' phones. Even though they didn't advance to finals at the competition the day before, they earned enough points during the season to qualify for State. God "turned it around" and the following weekend, our women's varsity show choir took third place in the state competition, a first for our school! One little worship song opened my mind to more possibilities. Worship helped me pray for something that I did not even think was possible. A lot more to come on this in the pages ahead; God was building up my faith because it would be a year later that I would pray "Turn it Around" again.

With all these stories, you might assume that my kids have amazing prayer lives. To tell you the truth, I really don't know. My children knew that I prayed, but they rarely heard my prayers. They weren't in my room when I was crying or confessing or pleading or doubting. That was almost always just between me and my object of worship, Jesus. I had a young mom recently ask me how I taught my kids to pray. I was at a loss. I don't think I ever did. Whatever prayer life my children have is due to our church, their youth groups, and their mission trip leaders. That is who really taught my children to pray and gave them a safe place to practice prayer.

Remember in the chapter Freedom, I said that sometimes God is extra gracious to us and lets us see a little more? This is no different. I may not know what my kids' prayer lives are like, but He has given me glimpses that prove to me that He continues to walk with my children. When Jon was about 15 years old, I was recovering from a very painful surgery. The first five days at home were much more difficult than I had anticipated. This was the first time the kids really saw me down and suffering. Dinner was delivered to me on the couch in those difficult days of recovery. Before eating one evening, Jon spontaneously prayed over me. He said out loud the faith that he saw in me and thanked God for my example. I never sat down and taught him, but Jon was learning!

Then there was Rebecca's courage—she really is one of the most courageous women I know. She had a college friend who was very far from God and wrapped up in self-destructive behaviors. But, when a weak spot was revealed in her friend's armor against God, Rebecca asked if she could pray for her, remembering that sometimes people are in our lives for that reason alone. The friend said yes, and Rebecca bravely prayed aloud for her right then and there. Although her friend couldn't remember much the next day, Rebecca trusted that God used her prayer.

Our kids don't live with us full-time anymore. However, when we are at church together, I have seen their response in worship, and I have heard their conversations. They, too, are discovering how Scripture and worship music can reset their thinking and ground them in God's faithfulness. It has given them courage when God's instructions are difficult. It has redirected them as their futures change and unfold, especially when plans and dreams get readjusted. Maybe I didn't intentionally teach them to pray, to use the Scriptures, or to worship even when it's difficult, but, apparently, they were watching.

What I have learned is that with each passing year, I have less and less control of my kids' worlds. At the end of the day, all I can do is pray. I really have nothing else to offer. I cannot protect, or fix, or demand things to go the way that I want. But I can lean into God and pray. There is no guidebook. It's an adventure—with a lot of course correction. Prayer is organic, specially created by the One I worship and my unique self. For that reason, I encourage you to discover your own relationship with the Almighty and not to compare it to someone else's. It will be as unique as you are.

My bottom line? *Amy - speak less, listen more, pray hard, lean in, and trust your faithful God.*

Chapter 7

Into the Darkness

The light shines in the darkness, and the darkness can never extinguish it.

John 1:5

Deep breath, friend. This chapter may challenge you with questions that many people wrestle with. Is God good? Why do bad things happen? The world is very broken. Evil is everywhere, but somehow good and bad coexist. If I tried to drop theological bombs, this would be a very short chapter. Let's just talk about reality.

As Aaron and I were learning to follow Jesus, we decided that we would not lie to our children, even in the hard conversations. If they asked us a question, we wanted them to know that they would get the truth from us. We worked to give them the best age-appropriate answers we could, both in the big and the small things.

Let's start with the small things. Rebecca noticed the Tooth Fairy did not deliver one night; however, the money was miraculously there a couple hours later in the morning. My very discerning child straight up asked me, "Did you do it?" There I was, held in the moment of choice: play along and keep the fairy tale alive, or build trust with my seven-year-old darling? As gently as I could, I said, "Yes, Honey, I did." Feeling very deceived, she yelled, "Why would you trick me like that?" My heart shattered! Tricked? I wasn't trying to trick her. I pursued her as she stomped away to her room.

Even on my best day, I could have NEVER come up with what came out of my mouth as I cuddled up next to her. It had to be an act of God. I said, "Dad and I love you so much, and we love finding fun ways to celebrate big things in your life, like losing your baby teeth. We didn't want to trick you, we wanted to celebrate with you."

We sat in the moment and embraced that the Tooth Fairy was passing out of childhood reality. Rebecca and I were sad, but we had peace. A brick of trust was laid between us. We rose from the bed returning to the day. Within a couple minutes, that very intuitive child returned with confidence and resolve. She firmly walked down the hall, her hands perched square on her little hips. She challenged me with wide eyes and brows raised, demanding the truth with her body language, "…and Santa Claus?" Never would I have ever desired for her to grow up so fast and put behind the joy and mystery of the Tooth Fairy and Santa Claus, but in her heart, she knew life was not a fairy tale.

Truth in the bigger things had already come to Rebecca. The Tooth Fairy was NOT the first time we sat together and embraced terrible realities. The year before, Aaron and I found ourselves explaining the unthinkable.

Ali was a sweet child and a good friend to Rebecca. Near the end of first grade, Ali's family up and moved unexpectedly. No warning. No explanation. Rebecca was so sad that her friend had left and not said goodbye. I asked the teacher about it, but all she was able to say was that Ali's mom was in a rough situation and had to move. No more than a week later, we learned that an angry ex-boyfriend of the mom went to the house where she, Ali, and Ali's sister had fled to so abruptly. In a fit of rage, he murdered little Ali and her mom. The older sister had hidden until he left the house.

Darkness. Evil. How do you explain murder to a six-year-old? That we even had to was more than my heart and mind could take! Many parents just left it that Ali had moved away. Some told their children she died in a car accident. I don't blame them at all for their responses. They knew what's best for their children. For me, what could I say to my already fearful child who asked, "How did Ali die?"

"I'm sorry, Honey. Ali had someone in her life that was a very angry person. She did nothing wrong. It was not Ali's fault, but his anger killed her." Oh, Spirit of God, do not wound this child of mine!

He will not crush the weakest reed or put out a flickering candle.
Matthew 12:20

Rebecca asked a lot of questions about Jesus: we all did. There we sat in our grief and confusion, and wrestled with the belief that God is still good. Ali was undeserving of death. She was a good girl. Jesus loved Ali, and He took care of her—somehow. All the answers we want in life, we often simply don't get. This side of heaven, we continue to wrestle with darkness and light, good and evil. For us to raise children of character, we must face darkness, stay in the room of unanswered questions, endure, and believe that, God, in the end, will not disappoint.

We can rejoice, too, when we run into problems and trials, for we know that they help us develop endurance. And endurance develops strength of character, and character strengthens our confident hope of salvation. And this hope will not lead to disappointment. For we know how dearly God loves us, because he has given us the Holy Spirit to fill our hearts with his love.
Romans 5:3-5

Jonathon experienced evil and darkness in another way. He battled nightmares most of his young life. Even today, as a man, he could still share many of them in vivid detail. I could have told him, "It's just a dream. It's not real." But I would be telling a lie. Whatever comes through the mind during sleep, whether good or evil, sure does feel real. I know because I have dealt with nightmares and vivid dreams most of my life as well. If I were to tell my small boy that "it was just a dream and not real," I would also be shutting down one of the ways that God communicates with us. Simply search "dream" in the Bible, and you will find at least 113 references to God using dreams. I couldn't lie to him, and it would not bring the peace that we both really wanted. Only the truth can bring peace.

At about five years old, Jonathon came down the hall in the middle of the night—again. I walked him back to his bedroom, but I could NOT get him to pass the threshold of the door. He had a body of a five-year-old boy, but he was as strong as a grown man as we stood in the doorway. He would not budge. He said, "I won't go back in there! The witch is still floating by my window." Of course, I could not see what he so clearly could. But it's the truth that brings peace. So, I said to the darkness in the deep hours of the night, "Jonathon belongs to Jesus and you are not allowed here." Within moments my sweet boy walked back into his room without hesitation and fell right back to sleep.

For God, who said, "Let there be light in the darkness," has made this light shine in our hearts so we could know the glory of God that is seen in the face of Jesus Christ.

2 Corinthians 4:6

We worked through intimidating dreams and nightmares for years with Jonathon. The big switch came when another round of night terror was happening, and my son finally asked, "What can I do to make it stop?"

I answered, "Well, Honey, we can't keep the dreams from coming, but you can always ask Jesus into your dream while you're asleep, or you can ask Him to wake you up."

You don't have to believe me or my son, but if you ask either of us, we will say emphatically that, yes, it works. We have both had a dream "shift" us to safety when we've prayed. It's amazing; anyone can pray in their sleep. My sister told me once that our bodies might be asleep, but our spirits are still awake. Jonathon and I have both experienced Jesus waking us up from a night terror before the dream ended. The Holy Spirit has shown up to us in dreams without a describable face and removed us from the scene. Jon had a dream where a faceless, cloaked figure opened a door, where a door had not been before, and he and the faceless figure walked through the door together to safety. I, too, was once having a nightmare when a car appeared to me with an unknown figure who drove me away to safety. Maybe it is not logical, and neuroscience can argue with me, but love, and peace, and even truth, are not always logical, yet God is all those things! Glory to our limitless

God who cares for us even in the night and in the darkness.

A hard reality for me to accept is that I will never be able to fully protect my children at any age from the evil of this world. Whether it be spiritual activity that happens in the unseen, or the living, breathing darkness that happens in the lives of those we love, darkness is unavoidable. It may get really close, and really personal, but it is God who protects us. My job as Mom is to equip my children with the truth:

God is our refuge and strength, always ready to help in times of trouble. So we will not fear when earthquakes come and the mountains crumble into the sea. Let the oceans roar and foam. Let the mountains tremble as the waters surge! A river brings joy to the city of our God, the sacred home of the Most High. God dwells in that city; it cannot be destroyed. From the very break of day, God will protect it. The nations are in chaos, and their kingdoms crumble! God's voice thunders, and the earth melts!

Psalm 46:1-6

Into the Darkness

Tooth fairies and nightmares were only the beginning. Every little battle equipped us for the bigger one that lay ahead. However, we could have never imagined what we were about to walk through. Remember in Chapter 6, I mentioned it was Rebecca's junior year of high school that prayer would be utterly necessary? Buckle up, friend. This ride is about to get rough.

By October, we noticed Rebecca had a growing angst about show choir. This was strange because choir was what she loved. By this point, she had decided she would pursue a career in music education. Naturally, choir was what she talked about most of the time. But she began sharing less and less, and she avoided talking about what they were working on in class. Aaron and I couldn't put our finger on it, but something wasn't right with her, and show choir was the source.

A month later, in our unlit living room, what Rebecca had kept silent, gushed out. She had returned from a church retreat that apparently gave her the courage to say something. What was it that had bothered her so much? Back in September, Rebecca had been playing around with a friend's phone, when she inadvertently read an inappropriate text conversation between her friend and their trusted new choir director. The same male choir director who had led them to such great success the year prior. Rebecca omitted details with me, but information shot at me as though from a firehose. What she did share didn't sit right with me, either. Rebecca explained that once the director found out from her friend that Rebecca had seen the conversation, he texted her and apologized. He said the conversation was out of context, and he assured her that it would not happen again. In a fit of rage and disgust, Rebecca deleted the text immediately. For two months Rebecca had dealt with this secret alone, while her suspicions of him grew. But this night, sitting in our dark living room, silence was broken, and the darkness in the choir was coming into the light.

My growing daughter found herself in the middle of a very adult situation. Fortunately, Rebecca trusted me with the information. Let's take a pause here. I want to give you a moment to think about what you might do if you were in my shoes.

As I continue to tell you what happened, please remember these two truths at this moment in the story: 1) There was still a lot of missing information at this point. 2) Hindsight is 20/20. In addition to that, the critical thinking portion of the teenager's brain is still developing at age sixteen and seventeen. Facts easily become muddled or rearranged. At this point, I encouraged Rebecca to focus on being a good friend. I had to keep in mind that an adult's reputation and career were on the line. The information I had was entirely incomplete, so straight to prayer is where I went. I felt like all I could do was pray.

The day after Rebecca told me about the text, in the stillness of my room, my gut wrenched sideways, and I prayed repeatedly, *Lord God, reveal only what is necessary for full healing…Reveal only what is necessary for full healing.* Every day I prayed the same thing. Aaron and I worked to support Rebecca's mental health. The information I received was second-hand and out of context. I'm not even sure I could report anything since there was no evidence. The text was deleted from Rebecca's phone. There were no clear motives. It was hearsay. Every way I looked at it, the situation was dangerous, and it was delicate. So, day after day, the prayer continued, *Lord God, reveal only what is necessary for full healing.*

The thing about light breaking forth in the darkness is that it just reveals the gross stuff the darkness was hiding. Warning—it's only going to get even messier. A month later, final exams were taking place before Christmas break. A rumor started that the assistant choir director was called out of a rehearsal and didn't return. Then an email came from the school that a teacher was removed from the school grounds for "accusations of misconduct." A flash of the same headline hit the evening news.

We went into the two-week Christmas break with uncertainty and very few details. I called the principal, asking for insight. I wanted to know what to tell

Rebecca, but he was very guarded in his responses. "This IS the WORST thing a school can deal with" is all I got from him. Questions lurked and suspicions grew.

The Christmas holiday came and went. It was time to return to school for the second semester. A couple days before classes resumed, the parents—and *only* the parents—of the varsity girl's show choir were asked to come to a meeting in the choir room. The principal and superintendent of schools called the meeting. The purpose was to get more information. "If you have any information about him or the girls, please go to the police," the administrators said, implying that many girls could have been victims. But victims of what? Um, the parents wanted information too. Every question the parents asked got the same response: "Due to the integrity of the case, we cannot say." They just repeated the message that our children's safety was their top priority and that what he had done was the vilest of things a teacher can do.

Without knowing what had really happened, the gravity of the situation informed us that this was no small mistake or "misconduct." The administration implied that it all would become public soon. Parents asked if the principal or superintendent could email us before anything went public, so we could prepare our children. We were dismissed, not with information, but with a sick feeling that something big and bad was going on. I continued with great uncertainty and tears to pray, *Lord God, reveal only what is necessary for full healing. Only what is necessary for full healing. Only what is necessary for full healing.*

All the hopes of parental communication before anything went public vanished in an instant. The very next day was unprecedented frigid weather, and school was cancelled. Kids were at home on an extended Christmas break without anything to do. Then, out of nowhere, the teacher turned himself in. The news stations exploded. In the media chaos, they carelessly attached the charges against the Assistant Choir Director. Two separate families were pressing charges for sexual misconduct of an adult, in a role of authority, with minors; however, the police report also included graphic details of behaviors, as well as the initials of the female students. It didn't take long to figure out who was involved. The victims and their families were publicly exposed. In an outcry, a mom of one of the victims demanded the media remove the link to the police records.

Within a few hours the news stations corrected the link by omitting the students' initials and graphic details, but not before we, and others in our community, read the depth of the horrific darkness. It got to the point where my husband had to skip over the graphic nature while reading it aloud to me and Rebecca. He just couldn't vocalize it. During this reading, Rebecca learned of the other victim. This one had Rebecca undone. She came from a good home with intentional and involved parents. How could it have happened to her? Rebecca's pain was palpable.

Rebecca's resolve was growing. She immediately reached out to her friend who had had the garbage on her phone months before. She urged her to take her phone to the police and explain that the communication had happened several months ago between her and the adult offender. Her friend was reluctant, but eventually said she'd go talk to a police officer at the school. That didn't happen.

The cold lifted the next day, and students returned to school from winter break. Each choir, nine in total, was told to report directly to empty, unused classrooms, rather than their first period classes. Rebecca walked into the choir room and saw the school principal and the superintendent of schools. Also present was a representative from Prevail, an organization that works with victims of domestic violence and sexual assault.

Once everyone settled into their seats, one of the victims, whose information was temporarily posted in the breaking news, came into the room. In her hand, she held a letter that she read to her sisters in choir. Her parents were with her. Her dad never lifted his eyes from the floor, and her mom stood silent with tears streaming down her face. The family was pressing charges, and this young woman had a word to share. She was so very brave!! From her letter she read, "I'm not asking for forgiveness or pity; I just ask for your support. I know there are some in this room who were being baited, too. Tell an adult; it is not your burden to carry. It's scary, but you will feel better."

Both the girl and her mom urged other girls to come forward. The students were then released to either go home with an excused absence or to return to class. They could choose what was best for them.

Rebecca was done! Her heart was shattered, and her mind was racing. She was swimming with anger and confusion, and she couldn't take it anymore. Rebecca returned home before 9 a.m. and told us all that had happened. Yes, we were very grateful that our daughter had not been baited, lured, or victimized, but she was traumatized nonetheless. She knew the dark side of this man that most, including parents, thought could do no wrong. This was our new reality. Evil stories reserved for the evening news were now personal and darkening the faces of the people that we loved very much.

There are innumerable responses that can come following trauma, all valid, and all a part of the healing process. Trauma can render us frozen or prone to outbursts of anger, and everything in between. But for Rebecca, after months of secrecy and silence, I watched the light of Christ and the justice and the mercy of God rise up in her. Clarity and resolve overtook her. Without further discussion or hesitation, she emphatically said, "We're going! We're going to the police! Right now!"

She had carried what seemed like benign, although weird, information for three months. The friend with the inappropriate text did not go to the police for herself. Rebecca was going to give voice to someone who should not remain silent any longer. Shaking and afraid, but full of resolve, my daughter got in the car with me and her dad. Within ten minutes of her decision, we were in a small comfortable room where a police officer took all of Rebecca's information, including what she saw on her friend's phone. Rebecca turned her own cell phone over to the detectives so they could download all communication that she had. Police forensics can recover most everything, even the items that Rebecca had deleted. The burden and deep concern for her friend that she had carried for more than three months was finally in the hands of people who could help. Within a couple hours the police contacted the friend and had her at Prevail for counseling. Her parents were also receiving resources so they could help their daughter. The days, weeks, and months that followed were filled with tears, prayer, and efforts to stitch back together a shattered world and many shattered lives.

The issues I prayed through were overwhelming. I daily asked God how to walk with my daughter. I was praying for all the choir girls: the ones he got his hands on, the ones he was "grooming," and the rest of the students and faculty who all felt betrayed by him. Included in my prayers was the perpetrator's wife. I couldn't imagine the shame and deceit she had to feel as well. Not only was her own heart broken, she was left to raise her little boys by herself. How would she answer them when they asked about their daddy? These boys were going to grow up without a father. This vile act of perversion and darkness tore apart lives, a lot of lives.

Months and months passed. The choir director was incarcerated for some time, but he was eventually let out on bail as he awaited trial. Girls were afraid of running into him in the community. Others still received cryptic communication from him while he was out on bail. During the summer, police discovered that he had broken probation by reaching out to students, and he was returned to jail until the trial.

Let's take another pause and address the issues in my own head. I had to deal with my relationship to the perpetrator. I volunteered a lot in the choir. I had had multiple conversations with him. I had encouraged him as he worked under the difficult head choir director. I had gushed over him, like all the others, for the success that he had brought to the girls' choir. I felt deceived. I

Into the Darkness

was disgusted by him now. He was a wolf in sheep's clothing. But there came a day when God asked of me the unthinkable: *What about him, Amy? Are you going to pray for him—and not that he'll rot in hell?* I went silent with God for a while. I was angry and disgusted. Now God was asking me to pray *for* the perpetrator. I didn't know if I could.

Then one day, during the summer between Rebecca's junior and senior years, God showed me His perspective on the matter. I was at our neighborhood pool. Having a full late-afternoon and evening ahead of me, I enjoyed summer relaxation while I could. Not many were at the pool, just a handful of nannies who brought the neighborhood kids to pass the day. I was lying on my stomach, half asleep. I could hear two sisters, Emily and Alli, as they were pestering each other relentlessly, like all young sisters do. Never looking at the scene, it all unfolded in my ears. Alli apparently crossed a line and hurt Emily. I heard the nanny intervene. She checked on mildly injured Emily, wrapped her in a beach towel, and comforted her. Then she talked to the offender, Alli. "You cannot treat your sister like that. It's completely unacceptable!"

Alli began to cry. The nanny scooped her up and said, "I love you, Alli, but you can't keep doing this."

God leaned in and whispered to my heart, *That's Me. What that man did was unacceptable, but I love him, too.* I couldn't breathe, and my eyes were hot with tears. With gall in my mouth, I did eventually pray for him. It did include a prayer for the full extent of the law to be executed on him for the sake of the healing of the young women involved. With God's new insight, the song I sang a year-plus before, "Turn It Around" would mean something more again. Turn around this horrible darkness. Turn around a life that deserves death. I confessed, *I don't want to have anything to do with the man, but, Lord God, please redeem him.*

The human mind wants details. We love information and closure. But we're not entitled to tidy endings. The assistant choir director was eventually sentenced to an unprecedented 16 years in prison. His wife divorced him and took their two very young sons with her. One of the victims that pressed charges finished the school year, but she had to take her classes in the guidance office due to the cruelty and bullying from other students. Soon afterwards she moved out of state. The victim who had had the courage to address her classmates to try and save others, graduated and moved on successfully to college. A few years later, I had the utter delight to witness her spontaneously come forward and be baptized at church while she was home from college for a weekend. I captured it on video and sent it to my daughter at school. Rebecca texted back that she was sobbing in her room, watching the video, so thankful for the healing God had done. As far as the friend Rebecca went to the police for, and the countless other students and parents, I don't where they are in the healing process, or how all this has changed their lives. I do know this: none of us are the same, and we never will be.

*This is the message we heard from Jesus and now declare to you:
God is light, and there is no darkness in him at all.*

1 John 1:5

While all that was going on with Rebecca, the darkness monster was devouring Jonathon in another way. The transition from eighth grade to freshman year was difficult for him. There were a series of difficult situations, both in the classroom and in relationships. Add to that, Aaron and I were unable to see all that Jonathon was going through. Jon was consumed by a battle that raged inside him. He had a lot of negativity attached to school and academics, and with good reason. Alongside the challenges of school were also deep, but unspoken, insecurities that rang in Jon's mind, echoing relentlessly. He was fighting a battle of lies. And Aaron and I failed to understand him.

Jon was struggling in an honors class, but we assumed it was just a lack of motivation on his part. He had a teacher whose style did not work well for him. She used public humiliation and harsh confrontation as a motivator. It wasn't until I bumped into a student at church who happened to be in his class. "I'm in Jon's Geography and World History class. The teacher is really, really hard on him." Sadly, it took her comment for me to recognize that he was telling us the truth; he wasn't just blaming a teacher. About this time, he also had a very darling young lady break up with him. This breakup hit him hard, which led to him running immediately to another girl who gave him too much attention. The new girl was not the type he would usually take an interest in. Even several of Rebecca's friends would say to me, "Mama Osgood, you gotta put a stop to that! She's not good for him."

For Jon, the pain and pressure of growing up, our expectations, and our lack of understanding, pushed him to the edge. Jon was swimming in depression. He fought against thoughts of running away and of suicide. Aaron and I tried to come around him and utilize every resource that we had. We had him tested through the school system. We kept communication open with him. We scheduled visits to a trusted counselor and kept him involved in his church small group. And we prayed. Oh, did we pray. It would be more than a year before Jon had his head above water, where he could begin to see the light.

Very few people knew the depths of Jonathon's struggle, or how the events with Rebecca's choir director affected her and our whole family. That's the thing with darkness. It's hard to see. We feel like Sandra Bullock in the movie *Bird Box*: fumbling around, afraid of being consumed by the very real and present darkness. After seasons like this, what I was left with was the bold clarification of my job. It is not my job to hide my children from the darkness. I needed to be there when the blindfold came off. I needed to equip them to believe in the God who is still good and who is able to lead them through all things!

Really, Amy—there's a rainbow in every snowflake? Yes, my friend, even during this season. The rainbow was in the growing trust and partnership with Rebecca. We could see a courageous leader emerging, committed to the truth. The rainbow was Jon discovering he is strong and has something to offer this world. And on the days he doesn't feel that way or can't perceive it, he has his God who will help him carry the heavy load.

Our family continues to wrestle with the reality that both victims AND perpetrators stand under the same truth. God's grace. God's mercy. God's forgiveness. Otherwise, the enemy wins and there are no stories of redemption. If those who are unforgivable are not forgiven, how can I be? If the wretched are not offered grace and mercy, will I receive grace and mercy? God overcomes the murderers, the deceivers, and the perverted with His perfect justice and mercy. God overcomes the hopeless with a hope and a future. God overcomes the nightmares with His light and His presence. God overcomes the wounded, the broken, the forgotten, and the harassed with His peace, His love, His comfort, and His healing.

And I will rescue you from both your own people and the Gentiles. Yes, I am sending you to the Gentiles to open their eyes, so they may turn from darkness to light and from the power of Satan to God. Then they will receive forgiveness for their sins and be given a place among God's people, who are set apart by faith in me.

Acts 26:17-18

Chapter 8

Letting Go

Some time later, God tested Abraham's faith. "Abraham!" God called. "Yes," he replied. "Here I am." "Take your son, your only son—yes, Isaac, whom you love so much—and go to the land of Moriah. Go and sacrifice him as a burnt offering on one of the mountains, which I will show you."

Genesis 22:1-2

"Code Adam! Code Adam!" Do you know this reference? This is the code retailers use on their radios when a young boy goes missing. When I heard it for the first time, it wasn't an Adam, it was MY Jonathon!

JCPenney was having a back-to-school sale in August. Jeans were buy one, get one for a penny! On our budget, I couldn't pass up this deal, so I packed my 4-year-old and 6-year-old into the van and headed to the mall. In all my life, I've never experienced a crowd of this magnitude, at least not while shopping. It was like Black Friday on steroids. JCPenney was so packed with shoppers that we had to go to the least-used set of dressing rooms, which were in the men's business suit section. I learned then that the kids weren't too young to be embarrassed by me. They were both mortified that I was going to go into the men's dressing room to help Jonathon try on a pair of jeans. Against my better judgment, I let my 4-year-old boy go in alone. He was thrilled to be treated like a man. I got down on one knee, eye to eye with my tot and gave him the following instructions: "Don't speak to anyone. I'll be right here. Come right out and show me the jeans."

That little stinker was really fast. He changed and came back out, shoeless and with jeans falling way past his heels, well before I had expected him to. I had turned my back, only for a second, to look at a shirt for Aaron. Although I could see the dressing room entrance, Jonathon couldn't see me over the racks of clothes. Remember, he's my adventuresome kiddo, so off he went to look for me. Instantly, he got turned around.

When too much time had passed, I yelled into the men's dressing room for him. And when there was no answer, I went rushing inside to find only his little flip flops and his wadded pair of shorts in the childless cubby. I knew Rebecca would not be able to keep up with me. I got down on one knee, placed my hands on her arms and sent a very clear message. I transferred my shaking fear to her, glared at her in the eyes and said, "Do NOT move from this spot. I will be right back! Trust me."

Thank God she's so obedient, besides she was as scared as I was, so she didn't move a muscle. I went several feet in each direction and yelled Jonathon's name. The sea of humanity and racks of clothing kept me from seeing anything. Then I was afraid that if I kept yelling in my panic, I would draw the attention of any kidnapper to the fact that my child was walking around like prey in JCPenney. I returned to Rebecca in seconds and took her by the hand. All the customer service people were busy at the cash registers, so as soon as a transaction was over, I cut in front and said, "I've lost my 4-year-old son. He has on a red t-shirt, no shoes, and he is wearing store jeans that are too long."

All through the store I heard walkie talkies echoing, "Code Adam. 4. Red shirt. Shoeless."

In the children's section: "Code Adam. 4. Red shirt. Shoeless."

In housewares: "Code Adam. 4. Red shirt. Shoeless."

In the men's department: "Code Adam. 4. Red shirt. Shoeless."

Seconds later, Jonathon walked up with a police officer. Everything else from that point was a blur. I hope I said thank you to the employees and to the officer, but my mama-mojo was haywire, and I cannot recall anything beyond being rejoined with Jonathon. Fortunately, despite his fear, he didn't panic. Jonathon went straight to the police officer on his own. This entire event was over in less than seven minutes. We weren't separated by hours or days, just minutes. But it felt like a lifetime.

I will give you a minute to process before moving on. I am confident that you are sensible and responsible. Just remember, from behind a book it's easy to think what I should and should not have done, to which I agree. But I was just doing the best that I could. I should never have let him go into a dressing room alone at his age. I should not have turned my back even for a second from that dressing room entrance. I should not have walked away from my daughter. I am fully aware of all these errors, trust me. I did not have a quick or easy recovery when I realized all of the things that *could have* gone even worse. I could have lost him forever, and it would have been my fault. But like you, I was doing the best I could. God's grace is abundant!

From the moment my children were born, the process began: the process of trusting God and letting go. Whether it was the first time I let someone else hold them, or left them with a babysitter, or sent them on the school bus, I have forever been in the process of letting go. When I was a young and newly married woman, I heard a mother say her little boy was on loan from God. Easy to say, hard to live.

After I had been volunteering in our middle school ministry for five years at our church, the group of students I had started with were about to graduate high school. My children and I sat in our seats for graduation weekend. Our church celebrates the students who are graduating from high school with a beautiful video that displays each graduate's baby picture next to his or her senior picture. My kids' little bottoms were still small enough to share a seat and squish up next to me. The video scrolled as my arm kept them tucked against my waist. The faces of the young women I had had in small group way back in middle school flashed on the screen. I was overwhelmed. These young ladies were graduating already? It was a privilege of sharing their world for a couple years. It struck me that, too soon, it would be my kids in middle school and then graduating from high school. I had the deep conviction that Aaron and I couldn't do this parenting thing alone. It became crystal clear that my children needed other adults in their lives. My voice alone would never be enough. They were going to need small group leaders, teachers, coaches, neighbors, and mentors. Not only that, I was going to have to trust those other voices to speak truth, hope, correction, and encouragement to them.

Letting go of my children happened in baby steps. Each step got a little bigger and a little riskier. Letting them be cared for by a babysitter. Letting them go to school for an entire day. Letting them go to their first sleepover. Letting them go out after dark in the neighborhood. Letting them go to camp. Letting them go on a retreat or a mission trip. Letting them drive by themselves. Letting them move away from home. Whether it's leaving your baby for a couple of hours to go to the store or moving them into college, it is a big deal. It will always be a big deal.

When they were still babies (at least babies in my mind) they had the opportunity to attend a weeklong overnight Christian camp. OK, they weren't babies; they were exiting elementary school and transitioning to middle school. Regardless, everything was new. They had never set foot at this camp before. Rebecca only knew one friend, and Jonathon knew absolutely no one. Add to that, we would have no communication with our children for the entire week. Here are the things I was sure of: I KNEW that they wouldn't sleep the first night. I KNEW they would get homesick. I KNEW it would be a hard week for all of us. I felt all the knots return to my stomach just like when I was a child. I tried to warn them of all these things, but they wanted to go anyway.

The only "communication" we had was to visit the camp's website every day to see if there were any posted pictures of my angel babies. As you can imagine, each morning I scoured those photos just to get a glimpse of my children to make sure they were still alive and hopefully not looking completely miserable. Aaron and I tried to make the best of it by going out and dating one another again. But internally, it was brutal to think of what the kids were facing without me. It was a long five days.

At the end of the week we drove an hour and a half to pick them up. When we arrived at the end of camp celebration, I hardly recognized my children. They had grown up about two years in one week's time. They both had a new confidence that was visible. Of course, they had an amazing time, and they wouldn't shut up about their adventures all the way home. We asked if they wanted to go back again the next summer. Emphatically, they said YES!

I waited a few weeks for the camp adrenaline to wear off and then I asked Rebecca, "Did you ever get homesick?"

"Yes, Mom. (Insert eyeroll.) I didn't sleep the first night at all; the second night was a little better. The third day a friend got sick, and we all started talking about home. That was hard, but then I realized I would see you in two days."

I pressed further, "Really? After all that, are you sure you want to go back next summer?"

Letting Go

"Absolutely, Mom! I know it'll be hard, but there's so much great stuff that outweighs the hard stuff."

God would remind me of this conversation time and time again. He has used her words "the great stuff outweighs the hard stuff" to me nearly every time I'm faced with something I don't want to go through. Letting go. Surrendering. It is something I have to do every day. Let's face it. At the heart, it's fear. I have to wrestle with the questions: What or whom do I believe in? Where do I put my faith? Lots of people have faith. Faith that good will win over evil. Faith in money. Faith in knowledge. Faith in their own abilities.

Let's peal that onion, shall we? I've seen bad people get the upper hand. I've seen evil win. I've never been wealthy enough to have faith in money. I've never been smart enough to have faith in knowledge. I've never been so skilled at something that it would be worthy of exclusively placing my faith in it. By process of elimination, that left me to put my faith in God; however, it was really difficult for me to put my faith in someone I didn't know. It took time for me to believe that God is trustworthy. The foundation rests on believing two things: that He is Good, and that He is Able. This takes practice and paying attention. Fortunately, He continues to give me opportunity after opportunity to trust Him.

What opportunities are in front of you now? Is there something that God is asking you to trust Him with? Does it feel like a small thing? So small that you are tempted to explain and map out the answer? Or does it feel like a big thing? So big that you can't see any possible way of it working out? Trusting God is difficult, my friend! But read again the words of my daughter: "The great stuff outweighs the hard stuff."

Faith is believing it, but trust is LIVING it. Surrender and trust are the action steps. When I surrender, I am saying, *God, I believe You are good, that Your motives are for my best, and that You are for me.* When I surrender, I am also saying, *I believe You are able. You have the resources, the power, and the strength to intervene in my circumstances.* When

Letting Go

I surrender, I believe this so much that I am willing to give up my plans, my will, and my efforts. I let go.

Um. OK. Not always. I just want to scream because I know all those God statements to be true, but I don't think I'll ever master it. Each season of life, or new set of circumstances, brings me back to square one. Do I trust God? Do I live like He is *good* and that He is *able?* Rather than saying, "I let go," it's more accurate to say that each day I choose to declare, "I'm letting go," which better expresses the frequent, ongoing choice.

Take delight in the LORD, and he will give you your heart's desires. Commit everything you do to the LORD. Trust him, and he will help you. He will make your innocence radiate like the dawn, and the justice of your cause will shine like the noonday sun. Be still in the presence of the LORD, and wait patiently for him to act. Don't worry about evil people who prosper or fret about their wicked schemes.

Psalm 37:4-7

All the little surrenders along the way led me to my greatest revelation about letting go. It was Jon's senior year of high school. As I've mentioned before, he wanted to get into a distinguished musical theatre (MT) program, which are highly competitive. After being accepted into a university, the school then requires auditions to get directly admitted into their MT program. Most other college degrees allow a student a year of general studies before applying into a specific degree program. Not so with his dreams. Over the course of four months, kicked off by the unusual eye infection, he auditioned at five universities spanning five different states. After those four months of auditions, there was the waiting game. Some colleges required acceptance in the school before the student would hear their audition results. Other schools made us wait until March until ALL of their audition dates were held. There was one school that would tell the student's results within a week, but only if they did not make it into the program. This college put their "no's" out there right away. Otherwise, no news meant they would be on a waiting list and might not hear anything until April.

In early December, Jon auditioned at his top college choice. The day was cold but beautiful, and he was feeling good. As with all the other auditions, he learned and then performed a dance; he sang 32 bars of three songs; and he delivered his monologue. We drove home hopeful. One week later came the email: "Thank you, but you did not make the program. Best of luck in your endeavors." He was disappointed.

Jon may have been disappointed, but I was crushed. I was shattered. I was just *sure* that this particular school was the best fit for him. It was an excellent program. It was just the right distance from home. It was the perfect size. He loved everything about it. Jon received the email while he was at school, so he texted us the news. It was in this moment that the lightning bolt hit my brain—*I don't know what's best for my children*! I had spent all their lives knowing what was best for them: the best foods, the best teachers, the best activities. It was my job to know what was best for them. I mean, that's why you go to your mom, right? She knows what's best. Not anymore. This was his future, and my voice was quickly fading. God put me in my place. Jon has one God, and it's not me.

Apparently, I'm a slow learner. Only a few months later, Jon was accepted into three great Musical Theatre programs. We were really grateful to have the choices, but now it was decision time. I worked hard to keep my big mouth shut, and constantly battled myself to not press him for his thoughts and opinions. We all continued to pray that God would reveal the best school for him. Jon took a much-needed spring break trip to Florida with friends. He assured us he would make a decision before he got back. We prayed, but we had to trust God to make it clear. Honestly, friend, I totally thought God would show *me* which school was the best one for him. I was convinced God would let me in on His plans. There was no audible voice, but it felt like a nudge inside. I felt like God sat me down, put

Letting Go

His holy hands on my shoulders, and said: *This is between Me and Jon. I will tell him, not you.*

Sigh. Surrender and trust.

I don't get to be a part of God's private conversations with my kids. Many times on my parenting journey I got off course. I believed and acted like I was in charge. Truth is, I still do from time to time. With every passing day, I have to let go, trusting the kids and their loving Savior to figure it out—together. My place is on the sidelines. I occasionally might get called into their game and asked for an opinion, but mostly I'm a spectator now. As difficult as it is, I wouldn't want it any other way. I'm letting go.

Then, calling the crowd to join his disciples, he said, "If any of you wants to be my follower, you must give up your own way, take up your cross, and follow me."

Mark 8:34

Chapter 9
But then God...

For the kind of sorrow God wants us to experience leads us away from sin and results in salvation. There's no regret for that kind of sorrow. But worldly sorrow, which lacks repentance, results in spiritual death.

2 Corinthians 7:10

I didn't take my kids to the park enough. And when I did, I actually told them to stop running. Let me say that again. I told my kids to stop running *at the park*—are you kidding me? There was too much TV and electronics and not enough interactive imaginary play. I didn't play when they wanted because my to-do list was more important. I didn't make the ordinary into glorious. I didn't cuddle enough. I didn't encourage them enough. I either didn't stand up to them enough, or I was unreasonable in my expectations of them. Too often I demanded that they change, yet I never showed them how. I held on when they needed to fly, and I let go when they needed me to hold them close. These things I know for sure. No one can convince me otherwise.

We all make mistakes, and most of us wish we would have done some things differently. But we also get to choose what we do with our mistakes.

I could just move on, shrug my shoulders and live with regret, or I could accept the invitation Jesus held for me: "Amy, take my hand and let's look together at why you do what you do." What was at the root of why I behaved the way I did? What did I think of myself? How did that impact my children? Was I motivated by my brokenness or by God's forgiveness? If I chose to move on without processing and live with regret, I would have never experienced what Jesus wanted to give me: Redemption.

Come close to God, and God will come close to you. Wash your hands, you sinners; purify your hearts, for your loyalty is divided between God and the world. Let there be tears for what you have done. Let there be sorrow and deep grief. Let there be sadness instead of laughter, and gloom instead of joy. Humble yourselves before the Lord, and he will lift you up in honor.

James 4:8-10

Sorrow is better than laughter, for sadness has a refining influence on us.

Ecclesiastes 7:3

Are you feeling crushed or accused? Do these verses seem too strong for you? Yes, they are bold, but they are true. I couldn't always hide behind good intentions. If I wanted to be free from the regret, I had to stop defending myself, and let God dig around in my heart. The truth is, I was fearful and selfish.

As William P. Young writes in *The Shack*, God and I had to pull the weeds from the garden in my soul.

One weed at a time, the Holy Spirit showed me what needed to go. He lovingly convicted me when I was out of line. The fear. Pull it up. The selfishness. Pull it up. Avoiding conversations because they were too hard.

Dig deeper. Bossy, controlling—these were all weeds. They choked out the beauty that God wanted to grow in my life. I saw my mistakes. I had worked hard to "fix myself," but it never worked.

I'm going to let Eustace from *The Chronicles of Narnia* book series explain what this was like, this process of allowing God to work in the garden of my heart. In the excerpt below from *The Voyage of the Dawn Treader*[9], Eustace, by his own error, became a dragon. Here he is telling his cousin, Edmund, what happened when he met Aslan the Lion (the Jesus figure in the series):

"...I looked up and saw the very last thing I expected: a huge lion coming slowly toward me. And one queer thing was that there was no moon last night, but there was moonlight where the lion was. So it came nearer and nearer. I was terribly afraid of it. You may think that, being a dragon, I could have knocked any lion out easily enough. But it wasn't that kind of fear. I wasn't afraid of it eating me, I was just afraid of it—if you can understand. Well, it came close up to me and looked straight into my eyes.

And I shut my eyes tight. But that wasn't any good because it told me to follow it."

"You mean it spoke?"

"I don't know. Now that you mention it, I don't think it did. But it told me all the same. And I knew I'd have to do what it told me, so I got up and followed it. And it led me a long way into the mountains...there was a garden—trees and fruit and everything. In the middle of it there was a well...The water was as clear as anything and I thought if I could get in there and bathe it would ease the pain in my leg. But the lion told me I must undress first... So I started scratching myself and my scales began coming off all over the place...But just as I was going to put my feet into the water I looked down and saw that they were all hard and rough and wrinkled and scaly just as they had been before...Then the lion said—but I don't know if it spoke— 'You will have to let me undress you.' I was afraid of his claws, I can tell you, but I was pretty nearly desperate now. So I just lay flat down on my back to let him do it. The very first tear he made was so deep that I thought it had gone right into my heart. And when he began pulling the skin off, it hurt worse than anything I've ever *felt. The only thing that made me able to bear it was just the pleasure of feeling the stuff peel off. You know—if you've ever picked the scab off a sore place. It hurts like billy-oh but it is such fun to see it coming away."*

"I know exactly what you mean," said Edmund.

"Well, he peeled the beastly stuff right off—just as I thought I'd done it myself the other three times, only they hadn't hurt—and there it was lying on the grass: only ever so much thicker, and darker, and more knobbly-looking than the others had been. And there was I as smooth and soft as a peeled switch and smaller than I had been. Then he caught hold of me—I didn't like that much for I was very tender underneath now that I'd no skin on—and threw me into the water. It smarted like anything but only for a moment. After that it became perfectly delicious and as soon as I started swimming and splashing I found that all the pain had gone from my arm. And then I saw why. I'd turned into a boy again."

Love is patient, love is kind. It does not envy, it does not boast, it is not proud. It does not dishonor others, it is not self-seeking, it is not easily angered, it keeps no record of wrongs. Love does not delight in evil but rejoices with the truth.   1 Corinthians 13:4-

After my own transformation from dragon to woman, I had to trust God's forgiveness and leave the past in the past. I still have some regrets, but God allowed me to try again. I found similar circumstances occurring in the present that were similar to ones from my past, again and again. If the same scenarios kept returning to you, would you think God is testing you? Would you think He is watching over you with His arms crossed, waiting for you to get it right? While I do see these as a type of "test," I don't believe He tests us to see if we will finally get it. I see it as God's grace. He presented me with an opportunity to try again. Not to prove to *Him* that I could do it better but to prove to *myself* that I could. He did this so I could see the victory and transformation that had already happened, glimpses of a tidier soul-garden.

How about some examples? It's much easier to see when the stories are told back-to-back, and all the muddiness of life is cleared away. It took me years to see these stories for what they were: Redemption.

From the moment my daughter was born, she was loud, and that's an understatement. In the delivery room, the nurse even said over my wailing baby, "Wow, they usually quiet down by now." Especially during naptime, she would fight and scream and cry, not wanting to be put to sleep. I would hold and rock her. She'd turn red in the face, arch her back, and wail. More often than not, naptime and bedtime had me red in the face, frustrated and crying as well. From infancy to toddlerhood, gentle rocking in a chair never got either of my kids to sleep. They were both held very firmly across my chest as I rocked and bounced from side to side rather vigorously. An onlooker would never believe that a child might fall asleep this way. I would sing what few hymns I remembered from childhood, mostly to keep me from losing it!

But then God…

When my kids were eight and six, we took in a struggling friend who needed safety for her two-year-old daughter and unborn son. My friend lived with us for a week while she took a rest from a husband who was deeply lost in his drug addiction. She greeted her toddler girl, "Good morning, little one" every morning before heading to work. Then I would take care of "little one" until my friend returned home. Their world was turned upside down, and they needed peace, routine, and provision. Little One's momma warned me that she didn't nap. But the world in which they lived had them so unraveled, and this darling tike just needed to rest. So here I was again, rocking and holding a screaming child fighting me at naptime. This was different than before, not because it wasn't my child, but because I knew God had forgiven me for not appreciating my own children when they were that age. This time, I sang praise songs over little one. I held on to her and didn't take her crying personally. I was more concerned for her and less concerned about my ego. God proved to me that not only had He had forgiven me, but He also restored the experience with my own children. He let me do it again, but this time it was the way I should have done it long ago. By day three, little one cried only a couple minutes before she was safely off to dreamland. And when she awoke, blonde curls tossed and wild, she would grin at me, wiggle up next to me, and ask for a snack.

Years later, God showed me something in my own growing children. As I mentioned in Chapter 6, Leaning In, I often pray during musical worship. Shortly after the kids returned home from their first mission trip, I was in a season loaded with parenting regret. Both kids were in high school and my mistakes just continued to pile up in my head. As the worship band pressed on with the music, I asked God, "Did I do anything right?" Through moist eyes, I cracked one open and looked down the row at my kids. They were fully engaged in the worship experience, oblivious to the world around them. I noticed that both of them were rocking side to side in identical motion. Instantly, I recognized it. That rocking motion. It was the exact motion I used when I stood in their bedrooms and rocked them to sleep. In that moment God showed me that He took those exasperated nights before they could even have a memory and turned it into a familiar expression of comfort, and they worshipped Him with it. That is redemption.

As our little Rebecca grew, the crying associated with sleep subsided but the loudness did not. She played loud. She sang loud. She talked loud. Aaron and I rolled our eyes and said to one another, "She does not understand her volume. The kid can't whisper." As a self-absorbed mother, concerned by what other people would think, I *constantly* shushed her. I shushed her at the grocery. I shushed her at playdates. I shushed her in church. I shushed her in the car. I shushed her at the park. Yes, I shushed a child at the park—she was outside! I can't think of a time when I just let her be her, even if it meant being loud. Of course, children need to be taught appropriate behaviors for various environments. I was excessive.

But then God…

But then God…

During Rebecca's senior year of high school, before she was accepted into the college program of her dreams, we went to the university for a private voice lesson with a professor. During the hour-long session, the professor tried to get Rebecca to loosen up and to have freedom in her breathing as she sang. The professor said, "Loudly, say 'whee', blowing all the air out of your belly."

"Louder!"

"Whee!"

"Ok, try again, whee! Let it out, louder!"

Joyfully encouraging Rebecca, the professor continued.

"Again, think about being on the swing at the playground, whee. . ."

WHAM! The professor might as well have slapped me in the face. Tears stung my eyes, and my throat tightened. I sat in the corner of the room, staring at the result of my sin. The conviction of my thoughts sent me spinning. I wanted to shout at the professor: "I shushed her in the park! She wasn't allowed to scream "whee" from the swing! It's all my fault!"

I realized that in my desire for Rebecca to be quiet as a child, I could have silenced her. *Did I plant a seed that her voice didn't matter and shouldn't be heard? Did I make her paranoid about drawing attention to herself?* On and on it went inside my head…

At the end of our campus visit, I had nothing left to do but to confess to her: "You know why it felt weird to loudly breathe 'whee'? It's because I shushed you all the time when you were little. I am so sorry. I never should have tried to contain you or your voice."

When she was a toddler, it didn't seem like a big deal. But looking at my 17-year-old daughter, the last thing I wanted her to believe was that her voice didn't matter. I wanted her to know that she has a voice that needs to be heard, and I would not hold her back from expressing herself. God gave me the opportunity to both ask her for forgiveness and to right a wrong. God redeemed my mistakes. Rebecca has found her voice and is now using it to speak into the lives of middle and high school students. And she does not sit quietly when it comes to issues of injustice. That's redemption.

Where Rebecca brought volume, Jonathon brought curiosity and impulsiveness. He was fearless in discovery. This led to outlandish ideas and attempts at things he was never meant to do. I will not go into detail about the emergency room visits (visits—that's plural). To expand on those would sidetrack me from my point. Instead, I'll share this image:

When he was three years old, we moved into our new home. The previous owners had left behind their pool table. Our house rules were pretty simple to maintain dignity and safety: get dressed (both kids had an "underwear only" phase), no food, drinks or toys on the pool table, and, most definitely, no playing with the pool cues without an adult present. Not long after the move, I went down to the basement to find Jonathon standing smack in the middle of the pool table wearing nothing but his Thomas the Tank Engine underwear, with his sippy cup and matchbox cars tossed at his feet, and in his hands—a pool cue—which he was jabbing straight up and down into the ceiling tiles. Every rule was broken in one swift moment. Jonathon always chose adventure.

"Stop!" and "Put that down!" were frequent commands from my mouth and not just with flagrant fouls like the pool table incident. He wanted to try everything, and my knee-jerk reaction was always "no." This likely went beyond common sense and safety. I stifled his growing mind and spirit. My controlling words reached their zenith when he was sixteen. Every other year, our church performs large-scale musicals with and for the community in hopes of attracting people who might not normally be inclined to attend a church service. The spring of Jon's sophomore year, our church announced that they would present Disney's *Beauty and the Beast* that fall. Auditions were coming up, and Jon was interested in the show. The audition application asked for information like voice part, previous experience in other productions, and the role or roles for which that person was auditioning. As he was filling out the application, I told him, "Don't sign up to audition for the Beast; you don't have any acting experience." One could say I was just trying to protect him from disappointment. I knew in my heart I was trying to control him. I wanted to be the voice in his life telling him what he could and could not do.

But then God…

Did I really want my son to grow up believing that I didn't trust him? Was all he ever heard from me discouragement and limitations? Did I really want to send my son out into the world believing his ideas weren't good enough, that he shouldn't take risks? Of course not! But my words and actions proved otherwise. Jon took my advice and did not list the part of the Beast on his audition sheet.

However, the audition panel saw something I never could have seen myself. They not only saw his talent, but they saw his teachability. He was cast as the Beast. Jon grew more and more into the image of Christ during the rehearsals and through the production. It also changed our family forever; we have not been the same since. The whole experience Jon had with the musical got him over the hump of his battle with depression and the lies in his head. When the show was over, I told a couple people who were on the audition panel, "I feel like I finally got my son back."

Performing in *Beauty and the Beast* also set into motion the next steps for Jon to pursue musical theatre in college, and it opened me up to a world for him that I had never considered. Many times Jon had put his mind to something that I wasn't so sure about, but he always came out with greater knowledge and deeper, richer experiences. Now I get to follow his example. Jon continues *to lead me* to try new things, take risks, and to dive passionately into what interests me. That's redemption.

In the previous chapter, I told the story about the kids going to their weeklong church camp about 90 minutes away. What I left out was why it was so difficult for me to let them go. It was my own separation anxiety. I felt it all the time as a child, and I was pretty sure I passed it onto Rebecca and Jonathon. Watching the two of them return to the camp, regardless of their fears about being away, revealed to me that the separation curse was broken off of our family. Not that they don't still feel the fear, but they move through it. What rendered me powerless and frozen as a child, my children fought through. They did the things I never could have done at their age. A simple victory by going away to a church camp led them to mission trips and international travels. Sometimes, redemption is simply the next generation not being held back by the things that held their parents back.

My final story on the matter is a long one. God allowed me to witness redemption on a very large scale, not just in the tiny chambers of my heart. Remember in the chapter on prayer, I said that I believed that God strategically placed me with people or in organizations to pray? Well, He was about to show off!

Show choir! (Insert jazz-hands.) Our children's activities can fill up our calendars pretty quickly. But for Aaron and I, show choir wasn't just a time-buster, it became our ministry and, well, maybe, our addiction. Show choir consumed our lives for seven years if you include middle school. I'm going to provide some history so you can see how God was working even when it looked like He wasn't. For the next several paragraphs, picture me with mini space-buns in my hair and blue lipstick to match the student's costumes. That should spice up the details and confirm my commitment to Noblesville High School choir.

Rebecca joined show choir in eighth grade. The middle school choir program was excellent, competitive, and quite successful. This is what sparked and grew her love for show choir. As middle school came to a close for her, it had long been rumored that the high school choir was under poor leadership. Rebecca had a friend from her dance company that was in the high school choir. She told her, "You will never be as good as you are now, because the high school choir director won't let that happen."

I volunteered with a youth pastor who once said, "I don't have a problem with complainers. They just need to be willing to be a part of the solution." With that in mind, I knew I needed to pray for the director and the high school choir program. I also needed to be willing to help in the classroom, to chaperone events, to wash costumes, to decorate for performances, and to help fundraise. *Don't just complain,* I remembered. *Get involved and be a part of the solution.*

Rebecca entered the high school choir program that following year. The environment was toxic to say the least. There was poor communication, inconsistency, and plans changed constantly. Parents were frustrated and to top it off, the kids were not getting educated in music. This really set me off because, by this time, Rebecca was seriously considering becoming a music teacher. My daughter's future depended on a good foundation in music and positive examples of leadership, so I began praying for the directors who were currently there and the ones who had not yet been hired. Just like a dirty diaper, the staff needed to be changed.

Her sophomore year, when the new male assistant director was hired, there was hope. Finally, they were being taught, challenged and experiencing success; I thought God had answered my prayers. It was that assistant choir director, though, that ended up causing the pain I described in chapter seven. I thought my prayers were answered only to find myself praying in courtrooms and weeping for wounded young women. Even though the perpetrator was behind bars by Rebecca's senior year, the program was still under the same leadership that had been locked in place for years, and the program continued to be toxic and dysfunctional. Everyone, from the freshmen to the seniors, was trying to heal from tragedy and trauma, and yet they also still possessed their ongoing desire to be proud of their work. Choir is not any different than athletics. Other schools know which teams are good and which teams guarantee an easy victory. Fifteen years prior, our choir department was winning competitions and traveling out of state to perform, but now we had become somewhat of a laughingstock to surrounding schools.

Even after the talented assistant director was removed, which I was grateful for, I had no hope that the program would actually turn around under the head choir director. By the time Rebecca was a senior, Jon was a sophomore entering the same choir program. I continued to pray that the department would be a place where students could find their niche, their tribe, and to learn and experience success. These things are necessary for healthy adolescent development. I really believe that what happens in choir (or on a team) can have a positive impact on people for the rest of their lives. We had two more years, and, even though I prayed, I believed that if it ever became a healthy place, it would be long after my kids had graduated.

Just weeks before Rebecca's graduation, my phone started blowing up with messages from parents and students. The head choir director had resigned! She must have been miserable in her job. Parents were complaining; kids were unmotivated. I truly wished for her to find something she would enjoy and where she would find success. Praying for our now-former director for four years had softened my heart for her, and I desired God's best for her. After all that praying, without warning—snap—just like that, it was done.

We would soon have a new director, but I was tentative in my optimism. Would the choir program really turn around? Sure, someone new would come on board, but would he/she be better than the previous director? Chatter among the choir people went quiet for a few months. Bottom line, I prayed and prayed for God to bring someone who would lead and love those kids. There are no perfect humans, but the right people can be put in the right job at the right time for just the right season. Thankfully, that's exactly what happened. Mini space-buns and blue lipstick were definitely in order.

But then God…

A few weeks into Jon's junior year, the new director held a parent meeting. The auditorium was full of parents waiting for some sign that things would be different with our new director. Finally, someone asked what his goals were for the department. The new director replied that he didn't believe in rebuilding years. The students were good enough to win competitions now. He said what every parent already believed. They were good enough, just mismanaged. Two months later at the fall concert, we watched the same students perform, but they didn't sound the same. There was professionalism, there was joy, there was pride, and oh yes, EVERY one of the choirs sounded amazing. At the end of the concert, parents were crying. One turned to me and said, "I think they hired the right guy." In our final two years at the high school, the program grew and brought home multiple trophies and awards.

During the six years we were involved, the high school choir program went through two directors and four assistant directors. Those years were filled with pain, success, trauma, victory, chaos, and so many ups and downs it would make your head spin. Through all of this, I continued to volunteer, chaperone, wash and iron costumes, and hang out with students on the bus and in the hallways of various schools on competition days. The choir and its people continued to be my world and my ministry.

Volunteering in our school's choir program was how I served. Yes, work needed to be done to keep the program running. But it was the people that kept me coming back—the people were everything. This is where I got to know other parents I would not have normally met. I walked with new friends through divorce, through job troubles, through problems with their children. Don't even get me started on the students! Tears fall as I smile at the memories. Like a river finds a way to the ocean, the students found their way into my heart. It was a privilege, being allowed in their world. It was my joy to laugh with them, to encourage them, to hug them, to tell them they are known and seen. It was my honor to walk with some of them through breakups, family troubles, and college searches. My sincerest hope is that while I was a part of our choir program that I was the hands and feet of Jesus. I may never have said His name, but it was my delight to love like Christ.

You may be wondering where God showed off. Our time in the choir program was coming to an end, and in a couple months, Jon would graduate. I would walk away from six years of choir knowing the program was finally under healthy leadership. Our new director was wrapping up his second year with us, and the new assistant director (our fourth!) was finishing her rookie year. They were a great complement to each other, and the students loved them both. The program had turned around so much that in just two years' time, the kids were competing at a national level. That should be enough to qualify as hope of redemption. But God did even more.

On the six-hour bus ride to the National Show Choir competition at the Grand 'Ole Opry in Nashville, Tennessee, I sat next to the assistant director. She told me her story, and God revealed how it fit into mine.

Kelsey never planned to teach high school but was grateful for the happy accident. In fact, she thought she was interviewing for a music teacher position in one of our elementary schools and only later discovered that it was for the high school position. She took on the attitude that God was leading her to something, something that she didn't know she needed. Kelsey surrendered to His direction. Then she began to tell me how after a few months into her new job at the high school, she realized that this was the school that had "the director that's now in jail." Ironically, this wasn't the first time she had taken a job that he had once worked in. It was his position that Kelsey had filled at her previous job at a recording studio. She had never met the perpetrator, but she knew his name, and she knew the damage that he had left behind, not only at our school but within other organizations as well.

Kelsey said, "I always wondered why I ended up places where he'd been."

I could barely keep myself together. I let the tears fall as I explained how God had asked me to pray for this choir department, as well as for each and every director that came through it. There we were, two women who were just being obedient to God's leading, now sitting next to each other, connecting the dots of God's handiwork. Because I took the Lord seriously about praying for the people He put in my path, unbeknownst to me, I had prayed for her through her schooling and job transitions. Could it be that God was multiplying my prayer of "whatever is necessary for full healing"? (Chapter 7) I thought the prayer was just for our situation. Was it also for Kelsey, as she brought God's love and healing to places that the old assistant director had been?

It was at the very last competition that I would ever attend with my tribe that God said, *See? I heard you from your first prayer. Give me time, and I will come through. I'm always doing more than you can see.*

My husband and I go back to watch the high school choir, even though we don't have children of our own in the program. No one sits in that audience with the same joy that I do. No one got to see the bigger picture like I got to see. I've enjoyed the fruit of God's work. What still blows me away today is that the God of the universe allowed me to participate with Him in His redemption stories. God is timeless and is always working things out.

Time. Redemption always takes time. Too often we give up on God. Mark Batterson says in his book, *Draw the Circle. A 40 Day Prayer Challenge*[10], "Our prayers never die. When we pray, our words exit the four dimensions of space and time because the God who answers them exists outside the dimensions He created. You never know when His timeless answer will reenter the atmosphere of our lives."

But then God…

I haven't always gotten it right. And I continue to make mistakes. I have two adult children. I've never had two adult children before, so I don't know what I'm doing. But God redeems my every mistake, my every failure, my every oversight. He redeems my adult children as well. God does this not only because He loves my kids but because He loves me.

Things may look hopeless. You may feel like God isn't listening or that your mistakes are too big and damaging. Leave some room for…but then God.

Chapter 10
Mama Osgood

And I am certain that God, who began the good work within you, will continue his work until it is finally finished on the day when Christ Jesus returns.

Philippians 1:6

God is far from done with me. Twenty years later and I'm right back where I started. I still don't have a business card. I might be a little wiser and a little more surrendered now, but there are no children at home for this stay-at-home mom. What will my "new normal" look like? I had no job to return to, no co-workers or projects to distract me. After moving our children into college, I went to my "work" for the day, but there was nothing for me to do. When the kids left, that also meant the choir was gone. No kids. No ministry.

I imagine that this is what retirement feels like. A lifetime of work and finding purpose and then it all just stops one day. No one dictates your time; you're free to do want you want to do. Sounds great, right? But there is also an emptiness that comes with this change. What do I do now? At least with retirement, one often gets a party or a farewell or nowadays, a socially distant parade. At the very least, handshakes and pats on the back usually happen. For me, it just ended. Everyone else's life goes on. The Monday after Rebecca moved into her campus apartment, and Jon moved into his dorm, I woke to nothing. There was a vacancy that couldn't be missed. Believe me, I wanted my kids to go. I missed them fiercely, but it was time for them to fly. It was right, and it was good. And I was happy to let them go and become who they are without me chirping in their ears all the time. But there was no party, no pats on the back. Instead of returning to the busyness of the kids' lives, Aaron returned to his home office, and I returned to my familiar quiet-time chair, alone with God. Really alone. The silence was palpable.

Some people told me, "You're done!" But I don't feel a sense of accomplishment. For me, there was grief, not relief. As the children were growing, I spent a lot of time wishing things away, believing "later" would be easier.

"When the baby can walk, it'll be easier."
"When they're on solid food,"
"When they can use their own words,"
"When they sleep through the night,"
"When they can put themselves to bed,"
"When they go to school,"
"When they can drive themselves," and on and on I went.

There are two important hang-ups with believing later will be better. One, I wished away precious time. Two, it's a lie. There is power in the present moment, and each present moment brings something necessary to my life. I might not like it, but that doesn't mean it's not valuable.

Mama Osgood

My children do not need me, at least not the way they used to. But they still need my prayers. They need me to listen. They need my advice, when it's asked for, and occasionally when it's not asked for. I am still Mom.

With the kids out of the house, they may be out of sight, but they are not out of mind. What decisions are they making? What are they running from? What is driving them? What is the enemy trying to lead them to? The bottom line is that it is their life to live, and I have to trust that one of these three options will play out:

> God will *protect* them *in* their circumstance.
> God will *deliver* them *out* of their circumstance.
> God will *redeem* their circumstances.

Whether it's their foolish mistakes or the wounds of this brutal world, God can make it right.

We will not hide these truths from our children; we will tell the next generation about the glorious deeds of the LORD, about his power and his mighty wonders.

Psalm 78:4

What is empty nesting like? Many people have asked me, and my response is not a short one. Allow me to illustrate it with a story.

From ages four to eighteen, Rebecca was part of a dance company. Each year, the studio would put on two ballet recitals, one in the spring and one in the winter. Our dance recitals were full-on ballet productions like *Sleeping Beauty*, *The Nutcracker*, and *Pandora's Box*. From when they were toddlers to graduating seniors, the dancers told timeless stories through music and dance. This was a significant part of our family life rhythm. The weeks leading up to the recitals were very busy for the volunteers. It was always a demanding season that included organizing ticket sales, costume alterations, the concession stand and novelty sales.

When Rebecca was fourteen, I was on the board of directors for the dance studio, so I had a lot of extra duties. On top of that, it was Christmas, which always translates to overtime for moms. Frankly, I was exhausted. All I wanted to do was escape. During this particular season, I was doing a Bible study with a friend. We were looking at the verse Matthew 11:28: "Then Jesus said, 'Come to me, all of you who are weary and carry heavy burdens, and I will give you rest.'" As I dug deeper into the scripture, I found in other sources that the word for "rest" used in the verse is similar to the word "intermission."

Intermission. The word was not lost on me. It was recital season. I knew what intermission meant. It means a pause in the action, so you can get up, stretch, get some refreshments, and use the bathroom. Intermission does not mean it's over. Act Two will begin soon. Empty nesting is intermission.

I am not done. Act One was raising my children while becoming a child of God. My Act Two will be practicing what I learned in Act One. But there will eventually be more characters added. There could be spouses for my children and the families they come from. There could be grandchildren. It may just be me, my husband and two children right now. Someday, however, it could be generations. My nest may be empty now, but there will be more people to love. I will be right back where I was, living and learning about humility, forgiveness, surrender and trust. There will be dark seasons in my own children's families when I will be challenged to believe that God is walking with them. I will watch them make mistakes, struggle with regret, and rejoice in redemption. Despite my best efforts, my adult children and their future families will experience many of the same things that I experienced.

Our children will also serve him. Future generations will hear about the wonders of the Lord. His righteous acts will be told to those not yet born. They will hear about everything he has done.
Psalm 22:30-31

"Amy, what do you do?" Here we go again. Back to the question that has plagued me most of my married life. It may not be on a business card, but I am Mama Osgood. Always have been. Always will be. I have mothered my own children, but I have also mothered their friends and other students who have moved in and out of our lives. I spent a lot of time looking at what I didn't have—a career and a business card to name a few. It took me a while to see it, but being a stay-at-home mom afforded me something special: the power of being there.

Nowhere special, just there, where my people are. As I said before, there is power and beauty in the present moment. One cold, dreary winter when the kids were five and three, I signed them up for swim lessons. Behind our neighborhood was Stony Creek Swim Center, a family-run aquatic center. It was the perfect answer for a cabin-fever-filled winter. The building had two pools at the time. If you were to look down from an aerial view, together the pools make the shape of an "L." Inside the "L" was the parent's viewing room with two large windows. I could watch both kids at once: Jonathon was on my left, and Rebecca was on my right.

One particular lesson, I watched Rebecca as she sat on the side of the pool. She gave me a wave, and then immediately leaned forward into her sitting dive. I watched her and gave a thumbs up when her wet face emerged from the water. With a slight turn to my left, I then looked and Jonathon was about to have his turn through the "obstacle course" designed for little ones. He gave a big wave to me and began. From time to time, he looked up to make sure I was still watching as he completed the floating obstacle course. When he was done, he climbed out and strutted across the edge of the pool to which I laughed and gave him a big thumbs up, too. This was it. It occurred to me: *I get to do this. When they look up, it's my face they see. I get a front row seat to their growing up.*

I have many memories of their faces looking up to see me, but that profound moment at the pool convinced me to pay attention. I may not have appreciated all the moments that were to come, but God gave me a poignant memory for each child as they transitioned out of our home. These memories of finality are precious to me and seared into my mind. I can still see their faces with my eyes wide open.

Rebecca's very last show choir competition was the state competition. Their performance was hands down the best one they had done that whole year; their poise, precision, and vocals soared. The senior girls felt great, and it was a good way to end their tumultuous journey together. Immediately after their performance, they returned to their assigned homeroom to change back into street clothes. As a chaperone, I waited outside the room in the hallway. The door opened, and Rebecca emerged with misty eyes and a huge, gorgeous smile. This. This right here. This fraction of a moment held a million different feelings for me. Her gaze met mine, and we both knew it all at once. These girls had experienced so much together. And now they had just performed their very best for the last time. This would not happen again. And I got to be there, not just that day, but all the days before. We had shared this. Sometimes the best thoughts and feelings are not held in words, they are held in pictures. I can still see her face in that moment, and, oh, that smile.

A little more than two years later, I had a similar moment when we moved Jon into college. He had the rare but fortunate opportunity to get to know his classmates before school started. The Director of the College of Theatre and Dance connected the incoming freshman class of 23 students through social media. By the time it was move-in day, Jon already had lots of friends. The whole day we were surrounded by friendly faces and helping hands. When Jon was settled, it was time for us to say goodbye. Each of us, Mom, Dad, and Sis, all took turns hugging Jon. Then, right before we left, we decided to go down a couple floors to the dorm room of his friends from church, an unexpected blessing. We had already said goodbye, but we all four huddled in the hallway near one of the girls' rooms. Someone grabbed Jon and said, "Hey, we've gotta meet so-and-so. Let's go." Jon turned to run down the hall. He took a couple steps and then stopped. He briefly paused and looked over his shoulder at me—a moment now frozen as a memory seared in my mind. Our eyes locked long enough for the silent message to be conveyed through a loving expression: "Go, you've got this. Thank you for letting me be a part of it." He smiled. I blew him a kiss and off he went.

All of our moments weren't glorious like those last two. Being present meant I was present for the ugly moments as well. I was there after school when a girl—the one Rebecca's had friends warned me about—broke up with Jon in a text, and he threw the phone across the floor. I was there when all three of us lay sick on the couch with a fever. I was there through the night terrors. I was there when a folder or iPad was left at home. I was there in the early morning hours before a show choir competition and the fake eyelashes wouldn't stay on or the hair wouldn't stay up. I was there when each of them was as mad as a hornet or as stubborn as a mule. Our moments weren't perfect, but I was there for most of them.

In those not-so-perfect moments, when life got hard, I didn't need to be delivered from my circumstances. I needed to be delivered from my perspective. I had to embrace that there is beauty in the dark shadows. Dark shades accentuate the colors, revealing an even richer beauty. I definitely didn't raise the Son of God like Mary, Mother of Jesus. But I understand the sentiment in Luke 2:19 (NIV): "But Mary treasured up all these things and pondered them in her heart." The good. The bad. The mundane. The spectacular. The unexplainable. I cherish them all.

Over time, I have come to see that God is loving me as I try to love my children. He, too, is the parent in the present moment. I fall short, but God parents perfectly. He is present when I acknowledge Him, when I thank Him, when I succeed, and when I feel good about myself. He is also present when I ignore Him. He is present when I am wounded, when I am stubborn, when I am wrong, when I am mean, when I feel insecure, and when I think I can rule the world. Just because I can't see Him doesn't mean He isn't present.

Mama Osgood

It has taken me decades to believe Romans 8:38-39 with all my heart:

> *And I am convinced that nothing can ever separate us from God's love. Neither death nor life, neither angels nor demons, neither our fears for today nor our worries about tomorrow-not even the powers of hell can separate us from God's love. No power in the sky above or earth below-indeed, nothing in all creation will ever be able to separate us from the love of God that is revealed in Christ Jesus our Lord.*

One of my most treasured descriptions of God is that of a goldsmith. The Goldsmith heats the gold, adjusting the heat of the fire. It is a tireless and intentional process. As the heat is applied, the impurities float to the top, and the Goldsmith swipes out the dross. The process takes a while. Not only does it take time, the Goldsmith *never looks away. His gaze is always on His gold.* Finally, when the impurities have been removed, the gold is ready to be molded into any shape the Goldsmith desires. How does the Goldsmith know when the gold is ready? When He can see His reflection.

There's a Rainbow in Every Snowflake

You rejoice in this, though now for a short time you have had to struggle in various trials so that the genuineness of your faith – more valuable than gold, which perishes though refined by fire – may result in praise, glory, and honor at the revelation of Jesus Christ.

1 Peter 1:6-7

The rainbows in the snowflakes are the ordinary moments. Vacations, big successes, and unforeseeable turnings of events are exciting, but the ordinary is where the beauty lies. The laughter at the dinner table. A walk through the neighborhood. A drive to the store. An unexpected conversation in the upstairs hallway. Rainbows. That's where they are, in the simple.

I wanted a title and a business card. God gave me so much more. He gave me people to love. My life has not been a waste. My life has been and will be spent on those around me, and it is completely worth it. About the time my identity stopped screaming for a title, I realized I didn't need it anymore. Being Mama Osgood is more than enough.

Just a few final thoughts before you close this book and move on. If you pass me in the grocery store or out for a walk and you have children dripping off of you, swarming you or running away from you, I see you. God sees you. You are known and loved. Moms, dads, grandparents, nannies, and caregivers, blessings to you. The struggle is real. But God is more real.

To you, precious reader and friend, thank you for spending time with me in my story. I pray that you have laughed, been encouraged, or at the very least, that you are grateful you're not as messed up as me. Now, go find God. He's been there all along. And He is writing your beautiful story.

Now all glory to God, who is able, through his mighty power at work within us, to accomplish infinitely more than we might ask or think. Glory to him in the church and in Christ Jesus through all generations forever and ever! Amen.

Ephesians 3:20-21

Epilogue

I did get a "real job." Three months after the kids moved out, I was hired by Creating Positive Relationships to be a part-time instructor. Two months later, I was trained and teaching in middle school and high school classrooms. I am privileged to teach and encourage the next generation in healthy relationship skills and decision-making, including how postponing sexual activity gives them the opportunity to discover who they are and to dream big about their futures. I love my job. You know what? I'm pretty good at it, too!

They triumphed over him (the enemy) by the blood of the Lamb and by the word of their testimony.
Revelation 12:11 (NIV)

Notes

1. LaHaye, T. and Jenkins, J. (1995). *Left Behind*. Wheaton, IL: Tydale House Publishers, Inc.
2. Tozer, A.W. (2006). *The Pursuit of God*. Camp Hill, PA: Wing Spread Publishers, pp. 11-12
3. Stott, John (2008). *Basic Christianity*. Downers Grove, IL: InterVarsity Press, pp. 17
4. Lewis, C.S. (2001). *Mere Christianity*. New York, NY. HaperCollins Publishers, pp.122
5. Moore, B. *Pride Poem*
6. Keller, T. (2012). *The Freedom of Self-Forgetfulness*. Leyland, England: 10Publishing Luskin, F. (n.d.).
7. *What is Forgiveness*. Retrieved from www.greatergood.berkeley.edu/topic/forgiveness/definition
8. Smith, E. (2004). *Breaking the Enemy's Grip*. Minneapolis, MN: Bethany House Publishers
9. Lewis, C.S. (1952). *The Voyage of the Dawn Treader*. London, England. Geoffrey Bles, pp. 108-109 THE VOYAGE OF THE DAWN TREADER by C.S. Lewis copyright © C.S. Lewis Pte. Ltd. 1952 Extract reprinted by permission
10. Batterson, M. (2012). *Draw the Circle*. Grand Rapids, MI: Zondervan, pp. 108

www.ingramcontent.com/pod-product-compliance
Lightning Source LLC
Chambersburg PA
CBHW021403290426
44108CB00010B/363